MOON

WALT DISNEY WORLD® & ORLANDO

JASON FERGUSON

Contents

Walt Disney World and Orlando's Theme Parks 7
History 10
Planning Your Time 11
Orientation 11

Walt Disney World 11
- **Magic Kingdom** 14
  - Main Street, U.S.A. 14
  - Adventureland 15
  - Liberty Square 16
  - Fantasyland 16
  - Mickey's Toontown Fair 17
  - Tomorrowland 18
  - Frontierland 19
  - Food 19
  - Special Events 20
- **Epcot** 20
  - Future World 20
  - World Showcase 23
  - Food 23
  - Special Events 24
- **Disney's Hollywood Studios** 24
  - Hollywood Boulevard 24
  - Animation Courtyard 25
  - Pixar Place 25
  - Backlot 26
  - Echo Lake 26
  - Sunset Boulevard 26
  - Food 27
  - Special Events 27
- **Animal Kingdom** 27
  - Discovery Island 28
  - Africa 28
  - Asia 28
  - Dinoland U.S.A. 29

- Camp Minnie-Mickey 29
- Rafiki's Planet Watch 29
- Food 29
- Special Attractions 30

Other Disney Resort Attractions . 30
- Blizzard Beach 30
- Typhoon Lagoon 30
- ESPN Wide World of Sports 30
- Richard Petty Driving Experience ... 30
- Golf Courses 30
- Spas 31
- Food 31

Downtown Disney 32
- Cirque du Soleil – La Nouba 33
- DisneyQuest 33
- Food 33
- Shopping 34

Accommodations 34

Dining near the Resort 36

Information and Services 37

Getting There 37
- By Air 37
- By Car 38

Getting Around 38

Universal Orlando Resort ... 39
- **Universal Studios Florida** 40
  - Hollywood 41
  - Production Central 41
  - New York 41
  - San Francisco/Amity 41
  - World Expo 41
  - KidZone 42
  - Food 42
  - Special Events 42
- **Islands of Adventure** 42
  - Marvel Super Hero Island 43
  - Toon Lagoon 44

Jurassic Park................44	Food......................55
The Lost Continent...........44	
Seuss Landing................44	**Metro Orlando and**
Food.........................44	**Central Florida**......58
Special Events...............45	
Universal CityWalk........45	History....................59
◖ Blue Man Group............45	**Planning Your Time**........ 61
Clubs and Bars..............46	**Orientation**............... 61
Food........................46	
Shopping....................46	**Sights**.................... 61
Accommodations............47	Orlando.................... 61
Dining near the Resort....47	Downtown Orlando........... 61
Information and Services..48	◖ Loch Haven Park..........64
Getting There.............48	ViMi District...............64
By Air......................48	**Winter Park and Maitland**..65
By Car......................48	◖ Downtown Winter Park.....65
Getting Around............48	Maitland "Cultural Corridor".....68
	Audubon Center for Birds of Prey....68
SeaWorld Orlando..........48	
SeaWorld Adventure Park...49	**Entertainment and Events**..69
Rides.......................49	◖ Nightlife................69
Shows.......................49	Downtown Orlando...........69
Animal Exhibits.............49	ViMi and Baldwin Park Area.....70
Food........................50	Winter Park and Maitland...70
Special Events..............50	**The Arts**................. 71
Aquatica..................50	Galleries.................. 71
Rides and Slides............50	Theater.................... 71
Food........................ 51	Movies..................... 71
◖ **Discovery Cove**......... 51	**Festivals**.................72
Information and Services..52	
Getting There and Around..52	**Shopping**..................72
By Air......................52	Orlando....................72
By Car......................52	Winter Park................73
	Mall at Millenia...........73
International Drive Area...52	
Attractions...............52	**Sports and Recreation**.....74
Wet 'n' Wild................52	**Parks**.....................74
Wonder Works................54	**Spectator Sports**..........75
Ripley's Believe It Or Not!.....54	**Golf**......................75
Accommodations............54	

Water Sports 75

Accommodations 76

Orlando 76
$50-100 76
$100-150 76
Over $200 76

Winter Park and Maitland 76
$100-150 76
$150-200 76

Food 77

Orlando 77
Winter Park and Maitland 79

Practicalities 81

Information and Services 81
Visitor Information 81
Media 81

Getting There 81
By Air 81
By Car 81

Getting Around 81

Central Florida 82

DeLand 82
Downtown DeLand 82
DeLeon Springs State Park 83
◖ Cassadaga 83
Accommodations 84
Food and Drink 84
Getting There and Around 84

◖ Mount Dora 84
Sights 84
Shopping 85
Accommodations 86
Food and Drink 86
Getting There and Around 86

WALT DISNEY WORLD® & ORLANDO

© GREG CRUDO

WALT DISNEY WORLD AND ORLANDO'S THEME PARKS

For most people, a visit to Florida is incomplete without a visit to Orlando's world-famous theme parks. Although the magic is decidedly skewed toward families, honeymooners and retirees also find much to love in the larger-than-life attractions.

The Walt Disney World Resort is, of course, the theme-park center of gravity in the area. Not only was it the first, it's still the largest and most popular by an order of magnitude. The resort encompasses four "kingdoms," each of which offer a distinct take on Disney's family-friendly charm. The Magic Kingdom was the first park built in Orlando by Walt Disney; it takes the fairytales-and-fun algorithm behind California's Disneyland and amplifies it into a self-contained universe filled with cartoon characters and immersive rides and attractions.

At Epcot, Disney's vision of a futuristic city has been supplanted by science-fact displays of technology, a "parade of nations"–style voyage through the food and culture of several different countries, and a selection of thrill rides that play off each of those themes. At Disney's Hollywood Studios, the magic of Disney is combined with the magic of the movies, while Disney's Animal Kingdom deftly blends live animal habitats, ecofriendly messages, and a handful of excellent rides. Beyond the four core "kingdoms," the resort also offers water parks, golfing, shopping, nightlife, and a wide array of dining and lodging options.

Although the folks at Disney's corporate offices would love it if you spent your entire vacation within their self-contained resort (and many people choose to do just that), there are

© JASON FERGUSON

HIGHLIGHTS

◖ **Magic Kingdom:** The heart of the Walt Disney World Resort, the Magic Kingdom is home to such icons as Cinderella's Castle, the Haunted Mansion, Space Mountain, and more. This was the first park built in Orlando, and for many people, it is synonymous with Disney World (page 14).

◖ **Animal Kingdom:** This is the most recent of all the kingdoms at the Walt Disney World Resort, and the combination of thrill rides, animal exhibits, and of course "Disney magic" has made it a wholly unique player on the theme-park stage (page 27).

◖ **Cirque du Soleil – La Nouba:** One of only three permanent Cirque du Soleil productions, *La Nouba* is a family-friendly exhibition of the Canadian circus troupe's innovative and mind-boggling combination of gymnastics, acrobatics, and choreographed humor (page 33).

◖ **Universal Studios Florida:** Although sister park Islands of Adventure boasts more coasters and thrills, the Hollywood-centric atmosphere of Universal's initial venture into Orlando offers a great combination of excitement (thanks to attractions like the Simpsons Ride) and entertainment (page 40).

◖ **Blue Man Group:** Universal has always been a few steps behind Disney when it comes to theme-park innovations, and for many people, the opening of a theater dedicated to New York performance art troupe Blue Man Group was seen as a direct response to the success of Cirque du Soleil at Downtown Disney. However, the Blue Man Group offers an entirely different experience, with a raucous rock-and-roll soundtrack and whimsical performances by those odd indigo mutes (page 45).

◖ **Discovery Cove:** Throughout the state of Florida – particularly in South Florida and the Keys – there are dozens of places that offer the opportunity for guests to experience up-close interactions with dolphins. None of them measure up to the sublime thrills offered up at Discovery Cove. Part island oasis, part eco-education center, and part pampering resort, a day here is utterly unlike any other experience in the area – dolphin, theme-park, or otherwise (page 51).

LOOK FOR ◖ TO FIND RECOMMENDED SIGHTS, ACTIVITIES, DINING, AND LODGING.

WALT DISNEY WORLD AND ORLANDO'S THEME PARKS   9

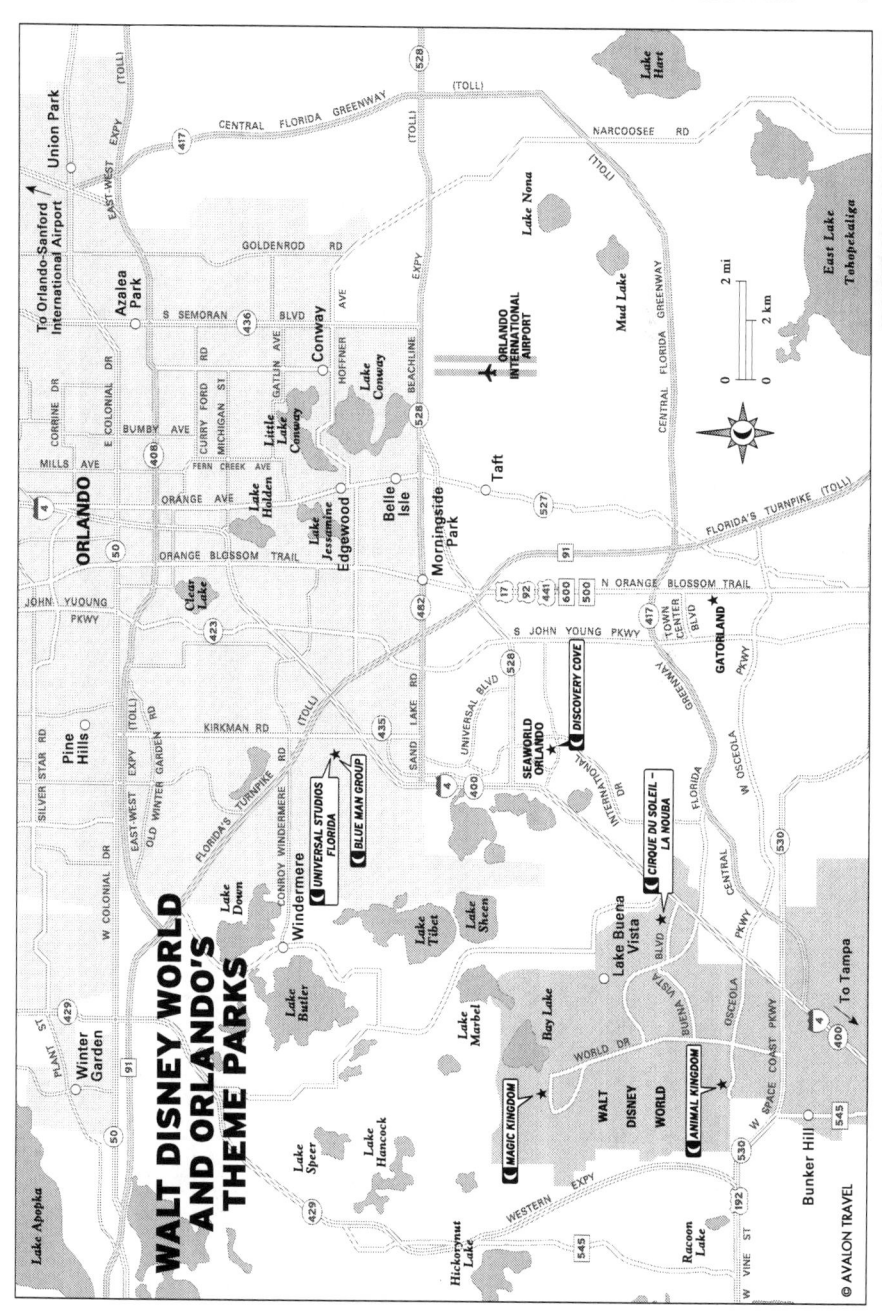

two other major theme-park resorts in the Orlando area. Universal Orlando contains two distinct parks; Universal Studios Orlando is a Hollywood-themed park, with movie displays and rides and attractions built around popular television shows and movies, while Islands of Adventure is pure amusement-park play with high-velocity coasters and thrill rides that still manage to pack in plenty of movie-studio synergy.

For years, SeaWorld Orlando was all but indistinguishable from its sister parks in San Antonio and San Diego, combining choreographed marine-mammal shows, sea-life exhibits, and a handful of decent if unspectacular thrill rides. Today, the main park at SeaWorld Orlando has expanded to include marquee coasters like Kraken, while the resort has also grown to include an excellent eco-minded water park in the form of Aquatica, as well as the exceptional Discovery Cove, which invites a limited number of daily guests for extended and close-up interactions with dolphins.

HISTORY

On October 23, 1964, a company called the Ayefour Corporation bought five acres of land southwest of Orlando. That was the first of many purchases made throughout the area by Ayefour and several other corporations that ultimately scooped up 27,400 acres of marshy and generally useless property. As it turned out, Ayefour—if you say it, it sounds like the name of the interstate highway that connects Tampa and Daytona via Orlando—was just one of the many dummy companies established by Walt Disney in the early 1960s. The idea was to quietly amass property and avoid land speculation for "The Florida Project," an attempt by Disney to build a large self-contained theme park and community unblemished by the unseemly commercialism that, in Walt's opinion, had sullied his original Disneyland park in California.

The "Florida Project" plans called for an amusement park—the Magic Kingdom—and a visionary futuristic city known as the Experimental Prototype Community of Tomorrow (EPCOT). Although the idea behind the original Epcot proved too ambitious, the Magic Kingdom opened on October 1, 1971, along with two hotels (the Contemporary and the Polynesian), a campground (Fort Wilderness), and two golf courses (the Palm and the Magnolia). Gatorland, which had pretty much been the main tourist attraction since 1949, was in for some serious competition.

With the opening and instant success of the Walt Disney World Resort, the Orlando area was instantly transformed from a slowly developing metropolitan area in Central Florida to one of the most popular vacation destinations for families on the East Coast. The resort itself has grown over the years to include three more "kingdoms"—Epcot Center (opened in 1982, the park maintained only a few vestiges of its future-city origins), Disney's Hollywood Studios (originally opened in 1989 as Disney-MGM Studios), and Animal Kingdom (opened in 1998)—as well as two water parks, a sports complex, two shopping districts, and 32 hotels.

Beyond the boundaries of Walt Disney World, the southern portion of Orlando was also irrevocably redefined by its success from an area of orange groves and marshes into the world's family-fun playground. SeaWorld opened in 1973, and for the next decade and a half, was considered more of a complement than a competitor for Disney's tourist dollars. With the opening of Universal Studios in 1990, the ante was raised. Disney rushed the opening of its own Hollywood-themed park to beat Universal to the punch, but rather than cannibalizing one another, the big parks managed a sort of critical mass. Universal's 1999 addition of Islands of Adventure, CityWalk, and its own roster of on-site hotels and shopping, along with the mid-2000s opening of a water park (Aquatica) and dolphin-interaction experience (Discovery Cove) at SeaWorld, have all proven to be successful in their own ways. And though Walt would likely blanch, the ticky-tacky tourist corridors that have sprung up along International Drive and in Kissimmee cater to the more than 50 million tourists who now flock to the area annually.

WALT DISNEY WORLD

PLANNING YOUR TIME

The seven major parks—the four Disney "kingdoms," the two Universal parks, and SeaWorld—each warrant at least a single day to explore. Trying to cram more than one into your day will not only be stressful and unrewarding, it will also be a decision that your feet will never forgive you for. Given the price of admission to the parks, it's best to get your money's worth out of each individual park.

If you've only got a day or two and have never been to Walt Disney World, that should be where you focus your efforts. The Magic Kingdom is an absolute must, and depending on the inclinations of your traveling companions, an additional day can be spent at your choice of any of the other kingdoms. If you've already been to the Magic Kingdom, any of the other Disney parks or either of the Universal parks can easily provide a day or two of excitement.

For trips that will last 3–5 days, allow yourself a day at each of Universal's parks, along with two days at Disney World and the remainder of your time checking out some of the lesser-known (and less expensive) attractions like Gatorland or splurging on a day swimming with the dolphins at Discovery Cove.

If you've got a week or more in the area and a relatively fat wallet, I would still advise against trying to take in Disney, Universal, and SeaWorld in one go. Instead, buy a multiday multipark pass from both Disney and Universal and alternate between them, taking time in between to check out some of what metropolitan Orlando and the rest of Central Florida has to offer, or heading to the coast for a day or so at the beach. Unless you and your companions are absolutely crazy about theme parks, the area has a lot more to offer beyond thrill rides and fantasy.

ORIENTATION

All of the main Orlando theme parks are southwest of downtown Orlando and are in relatively close proximity to one another. Walt Disney World is the most remote, about 25 miles southwest of downtown and 15 miles due west of Orlando International Airport. Universal Orlando and SeaWorld are about 10 miles southwest of downtown, along the International Drive corridor; these two parks are quite close to one another, with only about five miles of hotels and tourist-oriented restaurants and shops separating them. Worth noting: The town of Kissimmee, though relatively short on sights of its own, is known for its wide array of budget hotels, gift shops, and slightly corny dinner theaters; it's about 10 miles southwest of Orlando International Airport, making it relatively convenient for Disney-goers on a discount, although the 15-mile drive to the Universal/SeaWorld area is a bit more challenging.

Walt Disney World

When people say they're "going to Orlando," more often than not what they mean is that they're going to Walt Disney World. The expansive resort includes four individually themed amusement parks, a few dozen hotels, and a raft of other distractions, from water parks to shopping. The place holds a captivating spell over children, but the resort also caters to grown-up tastes with exceptional fine-dining experiences, luxurious spas, and even award-winning cocktails.

None of it comes cheap, though. Currently, the price of a single-day single-park admission to any of the four theme parks at Walt Disney World will set you back $75 (adults) or $63 (children 3–9). However, Disney offers a dizzying array of options that can bring the price of park admission down to around $25 a day. The "Magic Your Way" tickets allow admission to one park per day for each day of your ticket; the discounting is minimal at the two- and three-day level, but at $217.50

12 WALT DISNEY WORLD & ORLANDO

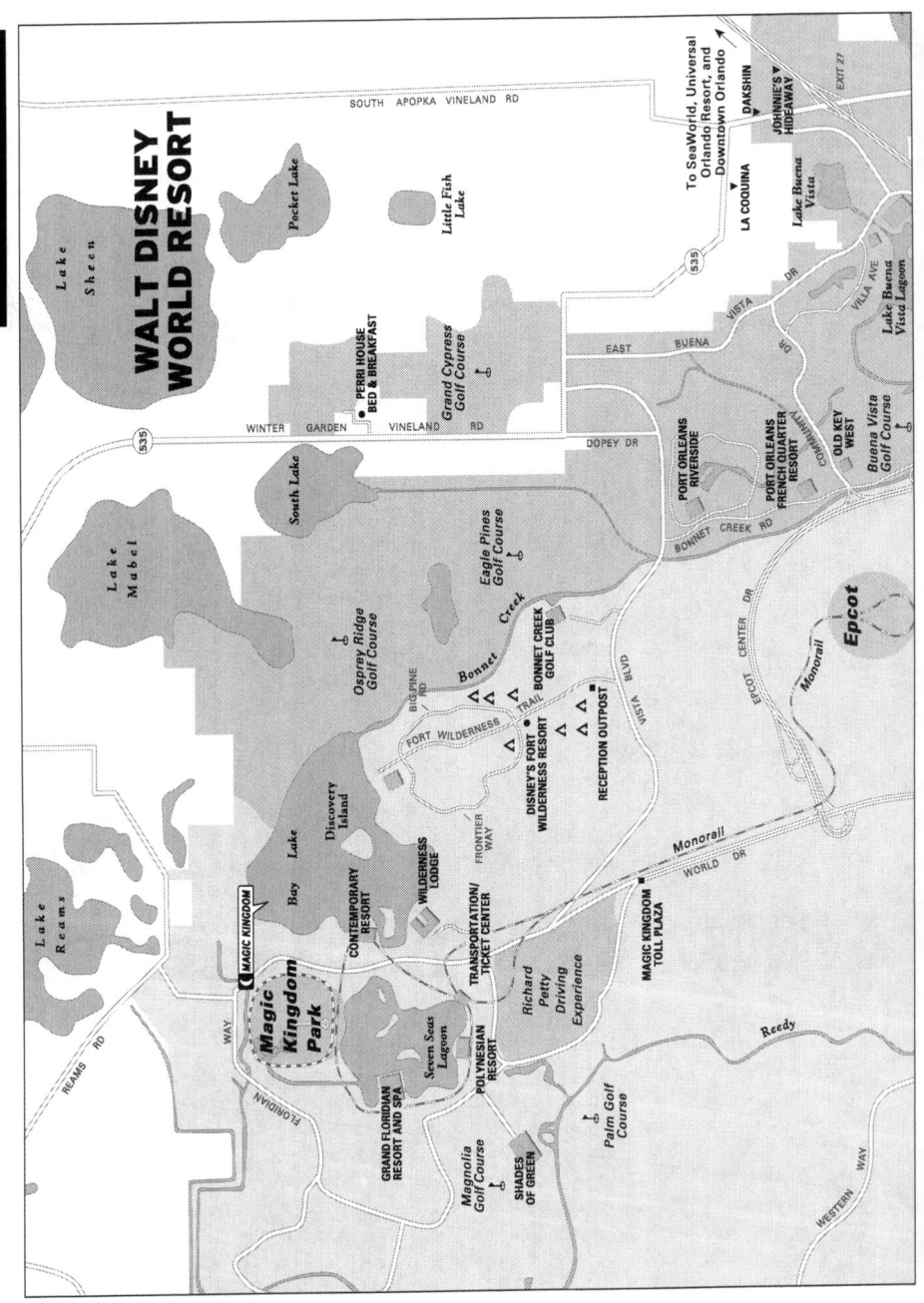

WALT DISNEY WORLD   13

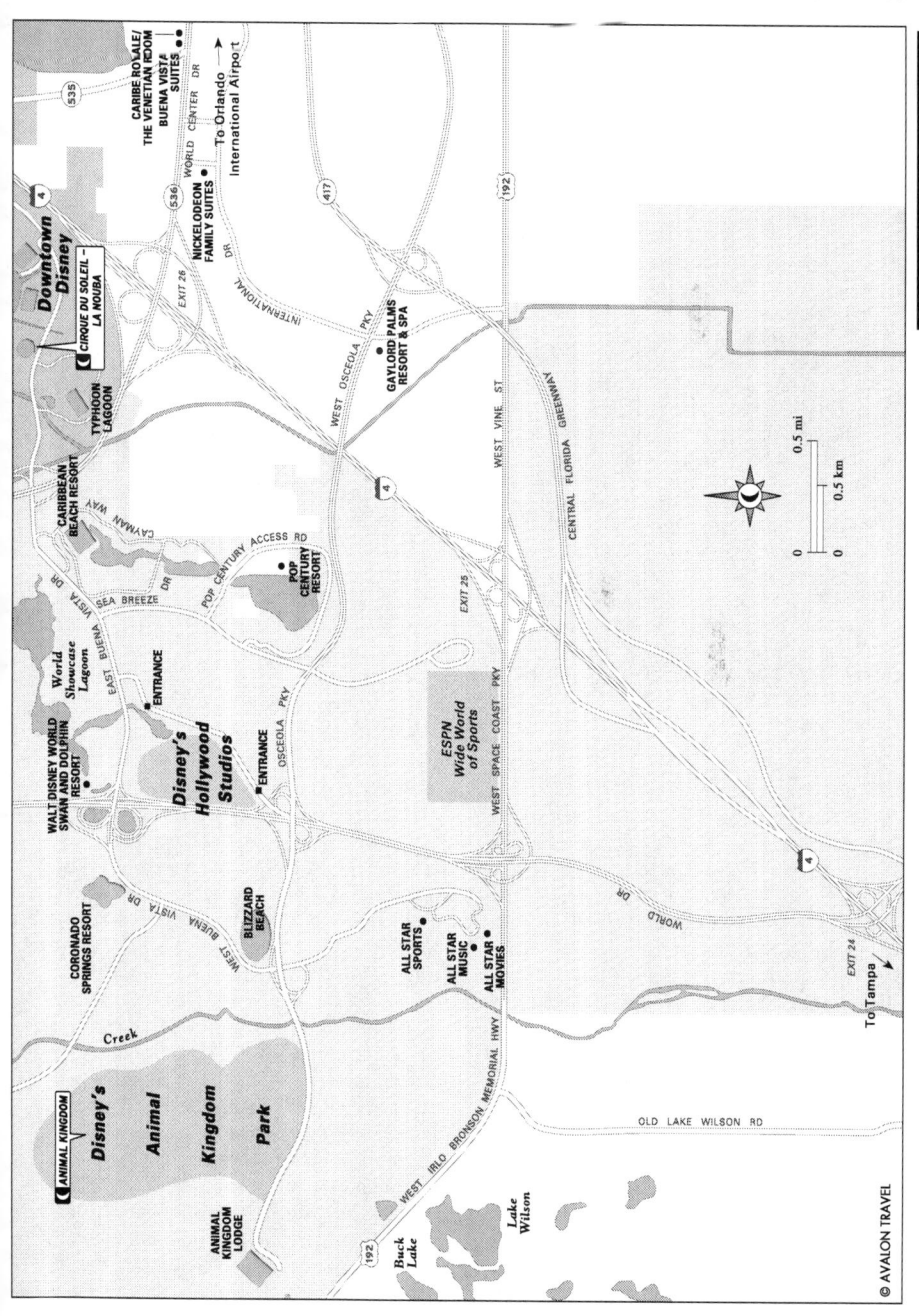

FASTPASS

Introduced in 1999, the FastPass system revolutionized theme park queue management with a very simple concept: show up early at the ride you want to ride, get a ticket with an appointment time (usually a window of about an hour), and then go do other stuff until it's time to ride the ride. Considering that many of Disney's marquee attractions present visitors with wait times of an hour or more, the FastPass greatly reduced the frustration felt by many visitors who left the parks thinking all their time had been spent in long lines for two-minute attractions. It also introduced brand-new levels of confusion: How much does it cost? (Nothing.) What if you miss your appointment? (You have to wait in the regular Standby line.) Why do I have to swipe my park admission ticket? (Because you can only have one FastPass at a time.) Ironically, the system has proved so successful that many of the high-profile rides run out of FastPasses by mid-afternoon, meaning that many park visitors wind up in the Standby line anyway; but the passes are still a good option for those who arrive early at the parks.

for a four-day ticket, you end up getting into each park for $54.75 per day for adults and $46 per day for children, and the pricing gets exponentially cheaper from there. For just a bit more—$237—you can get a 10-day pass. Keep in mind that the tickets expire 14 days after the first use, although you can add a no-expiration option for a surcharge of about 20 percent. Another option to consider is the "Park Hopper" (again, about 20 percent extra), which allows you interpark transfers throughout the day; this is great for people who are short on time, but also for visitors who want to, say, visit Animal Kingdom in the morning but see the fireworks at Epcot in the evening. Admission to the water parks can also be tacked on for an additional—and deeply discounted—fee.

For a truly unique Walt Disney World experience, guests can splurge on special access opportunities like the **Backstage Magic Tour** ($219), which gets you behind the scenes at the Magic Kingdom, Epcot, and Hollywood Studios for a guided seven-hour tour. Deluxe tour opportunities are available through Disney's **VIP Tour Services** ($175–215 per hour, plus admission, six-hour minimum), which not only gets you behind the scenes but, perhaps more importantly, gets you right to the front of the line at all of the attractions.

◉ MAGIC KINGDOM

The Magic Kingdom is what many people mean when they talk about going to Disney World. It's not only the resort's original park, it's also the one with the most signature attractions. From the spires of Cinderella Castle and the thrills of Space Mountain to meet-and-greets with Mickey Mouse and the halcyon Americana conjured up in Adventureland and Frontierland, this park most vividly bears the imprint of Walt Disney's clean-cut imaginative vision of what an American theme park should look, sound, and feel like.

Main Street, U.S.A.

The meticulous planning—and affection for a more innocent time—that was a fundamental element of Walt's vision for Walt Disney World is immediately apparent when you enter the park. The various hassles of parking, taking a tram, taking a monorail or boat, waiting in line, getting a ticket scanned, and passing through a turnstile all evaporate as soon as you make your way onto Main Street, U.S.A., a sort of trapped-in-amber re-creation of late-18th-century and early-19th-century Americana. It's no accident that this is the very first thing a guest sees on entering the Magic Kingdom, as the friendliness, cleanliness, and innocence of Main Street are every bit as fantasy-derived as Tinker Bell or Dumbo the flying elephant.

Vintage fire engines, "horseless carriages," and even an omnibus roam Main Street, and guests can hop aboard a trolley here to be ferried along the street to Cinderella Castle. Guests can also board the **Walt Disney World Railroad,** which circumnavigates the park

Cinderella Castle stands tall over Main Street, U.S.A., in the Magic Kingdom.

with stops at **Mickey's Toontown Fair** and **Frontierland.**

The primary purpose of this part of the park is mood-setting, and there's very little to do other than shop, which you could say is an appropriate mood-setter in and of itself. A couple of outlets, like an ice cream parlor and the enormous **Emporium** (at 17,000 square feet it's the largest gift shop in the Magic Kingdom), get the most attention, but there are a few truly unique places, like **The Chapeau** (monogrammed hats), **Engine Co. 71** (firefighter-themed gifts), and **Harmony Barber Shop,** where you can get an old-school shave-and-a-haircut as a for-real barbershop quartet sings along.

For the most part, though, guests just ooh and aah at the detailed buildings and the corny costumes and then weave their way through the crowds and the balloon-sellers to get to the rides and attractions in the rest of the park.

Adventureland

Once you've made your way up Main Street, U.S.A., hang a left at the photo-ready sculpture of Walt and Mickey and head toward Adventureland. As with all the other "Lands" of the Magic Kingdom, this area of the park is "themed" down to the smallest detail; the overriding concept is a reflection of the daydreams of a boy who can't get enough of matinee heroes and literary tales of adventure.

The **Swiss Family Treehouse** is based on the 1960 Disney film *The Swiss Family Robinson,* and much like the movie itself, this attraction's charms are...subtle. Simply put, you'll be walking up and back down a 90-foot-high manmade tree, gawking at the stranded family's survivalist inventions (a rope-and-pulley system used for hauling buckets of water, for example) and wondering what exactly the fuss is about. Most guests skip it, which is understandable, but not every attraction need be a cavalcade of lights and animatronics, and personally I think the Treehouse is sort of neat. My kids (and my wife, and everyone I've ever gone to Magic Kingdom with) vehemently disagree. If you're with someone who insists on ascending the tree but you'd rather not, or if you're physically disabled and unable to join him or her (this is the only nonaccessible attraction in the park), enjoy one of the best snacks in the entire Magic Kingdom: a Dole Whip soft-serve pineapple ice cream from the **Aloha Isle** snack bar.

Little ones will flock to the **Magic Carpets of Aladdin** ride, which is essentially a repainted version of the Dumbo ride in Fantasyland; four people get into a "carpet" and the carpets rotate around the big lamp in the center. Riders can control both the up-and-down motion of their "carpet" as well as the pitch. Not exactly inventive, this ride seems more appropriate for a local carnival than for the place where dreams are supposed to come true; the fact that it's a note-for-note copy of another ride in the same park makes it doubly disappointing.

The **Enchanted Tiki Room** was the first Disney attraction to fully incorporate animatronic technology, and it has been a nostalgic favorite for years. Copied over from Disneyland for Walt Disney World's opening in 1971, the Tiki Room was more of a show than an attraction, as animatronic tropical animals cracked awful jokes and sang songs in an environment thick with '60s exotica shtick. The 20-minute program was thoroughly overhauled in the last few years, and now elements from *The Lion King* and *Aladdin* have made their way into the show. The original four bird hosts are still on hand, though, and they still have the best zingers. Adults will enjoy the campiness of the entire routine, while somehow the jokes evoke massive belly laughs from the preteen set; those who fall in between those two categories will likely only be tempted by the lure of seats and ice-cold air-conditioning.

Like the Swiss Family Treehouse, the **Jungle Cruise** is an Adventureland attraction that seems like little more than a leftover from a long-ago time. In this age of Discovery Channel documentaries, ecotourism, and, well, Disney's Animal Kingdom, the thrill of seeing fake zebras, snakes, rhinos, and tigers is limited. Still, this slow-moving boat ride makes up for its lack of live animals with a stream of well-rehearsed and ultracorny jokes that issue forth from the mouth of your "tour guide." Still, in true Disney fashion the animatronic beasts are fairly realistic, and the well-choreographed river adventure is a sight to behold. Danger is around every corner as you make your way through four continents in 10 minutes, but you'll be laughing (or groaning) so much you'll hardly notice.

Oddly, before Johnny Depp smeared his eye makeup and boarded the *Black Pearl,* the **Pirates of the Caribbean** ride was often mentioned in the same breath as attractions like the Jungle Cruise or the Tiki Room. It was seen as little more than a fusty animatronic-heavy leftover from the park's opening, offering little more than nostalgia and a temporary air-conditioned reprieve from the Florida heat. Today, the ride has been lightly renovated to reflect its theatrical success, and several elements from the movie have been somewhat clumsily incorporated into it. But if you spend your time on the ride bemoaning the changes and playing "Spot Jack Sparrow" with your boatmates, you'll miss out on the essential reason for the attraction's enduring popularity: It's fun, it's a little thrilling, and it's even a little naughty. From the moment you board your boat and ride through the pirate battles and raids, the immersive genius of Disney's Imagineering team is evident; even the most seasoned park-hopper will get a thrill as their boat ascends a rapid and emerges onto a ship-to-ship battle, complete with cannon fire.

Liberty Square

The colonial-era theme of Liberty Square should make it a lot more exciting, but other than the hagiographic animatronics of **The Hall of Presidents,** there's little to do here but take snapshots of your loved ones in the stockade and grab a turkey leg on the way to other areas of the park.

The Haunted Mansion, though technically part of Liberty Square, doesn't fit in with the patriotic theme; still, as it is situated between Liberty Square and Fantasyland, one can only assume that the park's planners though it unwise to put all the ghosts and ghouls alongside Winnie the Pooh and Snow White. The mansion remains one of the Magic Kingdom's marquee attractions, and it's easy to understand why. Two-person "doom buggies" take guests on an eight-minute tour of this spook-infested mansion, from the ground floor to the attic. The sights along this ride are among the most intricately detailed in all of Walt Disney World, and from the wallpaper to the inscriptions on the headstones, there's always some new thing to notice. While inherently something of a scary experience—those graves aren't going to fill themselves—this ride has always managed to successfully balance thrills and humor, and while some of the gags are a little dark and others are a little corny, all but the most knock-kneed young one will be able to muster a laugh long enough to chase away their fears.

Fantasyland

When people think of Walt Disney World, they almost immediately envision Fantasyland. As home to the iconic **Cinderella Castle** as well as multiple rides and attractions built around beloved characters from decades of Disney movies, Fantasyland is the emotional heart that beats inside all the thrill rides, souvenir stands, and vendors of $3 water bottles in all the other areas of the resort. While certainly thick with its own peculiarly sneaky brand of consumerism, it must be noted that Fantasyland is the one "land" in the Magic Kingdom where the ratio of attractions-to-vendors seems almost reasonable. More than any other part of the park, Fantasyland is an essential stop on any Disney itinerary, whether or not you are traveling with young children.

Entering from Liberty Square and the Haunted Mansion, the first attraction is **It's a Small World**. As something of an eternal punch line, the ride itself has become instantly associated with a headache-inducing repetition of its cloyingly simplistic theme song. There are even anecdotal reports of people (in my family!) being driven to near panic-attack states by the song. I don't believe any of it. The ride is sweet, as slow-moving boats give riders a tour of happy children all over the world. Yes, every single one of those children is singing the song, but if it were ditched in favor of, say, Bob Marley's "One Love," can you imagine the outcry? And though it's simplistic, the message of universality at the ride's heart—the ride itself was built for inclusion at the UNICEF pavilion at the 1964 World's Fair—is hard to argue with. A recent renovation did little to alter the ride's fundamentals; instead, a much-needed fresh coat of paint was applied throughout, some of the "children's" costumes were refurbished, and the soundtrack was given improved fidelity. Check your cynicism at the door.

As famous or infamous as It's a Small World is, it's the character-themed rides in Fantasyland that are the biggest draw, and which usually have the longest lines. On the face of it, **Peter Pan's Flight, Snow White's Scary Adventures**, and **The Many Adventures of Winnie the Pooh** are little more than motion-enhanced retellings of the classic tales. But in true Disney fashion, all three of these rides are finely detailed and choreographed excursions that take riders deep into the story. The soaring sensation on Peter Pan's Flight, the deep-rooted terror brought on by the stepmother-to-wicked-witch transformation in the Snow White ride, and the goofy fun of riding around in one of Pooh's honey pots are immersive and highly enjoyable. Worth noting: The "scary" adjective in the title of the Snow White ride is not accidental; young children will likely be more scared on this attraction than in the Haunted Mansion.

In Fantasyland a clutch of traditional carnival rides are transformed into **Cinderella's Golden Carousel, Dumbo the Flying Elephant**, and the **Mad Tea Party**. None are especially innovative, but all of them—especially the spinning teacups of the Mad Tea Party—are fun.

Directly across from the Dumbo ride is **Pooh's Playful Spot,** a spacious themed playground that gives kids a chance to play in Rabbit's Garden, splash around in the Floody Place, clamber over giant logs, and poke around in Pooh's house.

Little ones will also get a kick out of **Storytime with Belle,** a 20-minute show where they can hear the *Beauty and the Beast* heroine tell the tale of, uh, *Beauty and the Beast.* In true Disney fashion, there's plenty of audience interaction and lots of songs.

Mickey's PhilharMagic is one of several 3-D movie experiences at the Walt Disney World Resort. It's also on the grandest scale: The theater houses the world's largest seamless movie screen. The movie itself is equally grandiose, incorporating almost a dozen classic Disney characters (from Mickey and Donald to Jasmine and Simba), sight gags, songs, and some very impressive 3-D effects.

Mickey's Toontown Fair

Despite the presence of a couple of kid-friendly rides—**Donald's Boat** is a water-squirting fun house, and **The Barnstormer** is a Goofy-themed rollercoaster—the main reason most folks make their way to Mickey's Toontown Fair is to line up for a walk through **Mickey's Country House,** because it's where the emblematic mouse "lives." Visitors get to see

MEETING DISNEY CHARACTERS

As soon as you enter the turnstiles of the Magic Kingdom, the very first gift shop you'll see is one that specializes in something that might seem peculiar for an amusement park: autograph books and pens. For children, and frankly, for many adults, spending the day gathering the signatures of characters like Mickey Mouse, Winnie the Pooh, Snow White, or even Captain Jack Sparrow is a time-honored pastime.

There are two ways to meet the characters: by accident, or on purpose. As you're strolling throughout the Magic Kingdom, you'll constantly be coming across throngs of children gathered around costumed characters and their handlers; simply get in line and wait your turn. In my opinion, this is the best way to approach the task, as the happenstance nature of the encounters only adds to the magical thrill your kids will get when you accidentally sight a beloved character.

There are scheduled appearances throughout the park during the day (consult the guide map), as well as opportunities to queue up in places like the **Toontown Hall of Fame** to encounter a cavalcade of characters. There are also "character dining" opportunities at several restaurants throughout the Magic Kingdom and other parks; reservations are essential for these, so consult your guide map for specific locations and call 407/WDW-DINE (407/939-3463) to reserve.

---

his bedroom and wardrobe full of identical tuxedoes, his outdoor workshop and garden (complete with doghouse for Pluto), and even his messy kitchen. But most importantly, at the end of the tour through the house, you get to see Mickey and even get an autograph. Predictably, lines are very long here, but getting to peek inside the private life of a 6-foot-tall mouse who's a movie star is well worth it.

Next door is **Minnie's Country House** (because, of course, these two aren't married), which is decked out in plenty of pink and frills. The setup is essentially the same as at Mickey's house, only with no regularly scheduled character meet-and-greet (although Minnie sometimes shows up in her backyard).

Tomorrowland

The retro-futuristic vibe at Tomorrowland was ratcheted up in the '90s to reflect the reality that Walt's '60s-era vision of the future was unlikely to come into fruition exactly as he saw it. This area of the park was themed to represent "the future that never was," a polished-chrome and rounded-edge future of rocket-ship cars envisioned by the sci-fi writers of the 1920s and 1930s. The theming is the most pronounced in attractions like **Tomorrowland Transit Authority** (a "people mover" that loops through Space Mountain, the Carousel of Progress, the Buzz Lightyear attraction, and other points throughout Tomorrowland) and the elevated spinning rockets of the **Astro Orbiter**.

Most people flock to Tomorrowland for one reason: **Space Mountain.** Opened in 1975, the 2.5-minute-long 28-mph indoor roller coaster ride is far from the fastest coaster around, but for years the combination of quirky futurism, quick turns, and darkened thrills has been irresistible to roller coaster fans. Space Mountain underwent a much-needed renovation in 2009. Lines stack up quickly here, so during high season a FastPass is essential.

Stitch's Great Escape! is simply a rebranded and toned-down update of an extremely intense theater-in-the-round attraction, "The ExtraTERRORestrial Alien Encounter." The new version puts the mischievous Stitch at center stage as a captured alien who breaks free; there's lots of darkness, startles, and alien spit in this one, but there are plenty of laughs to break the tension.

Monsters, Inc. Laugh Floor is a remarkable attraction. Based on the revelation of the titular film—in which the monsters discover that laughs, rather than screams, are more effective at producing the energy they need—there has been a comedy club set up that allows humans to come in and provide some laughs/fuel. The premise, however, isn't what makes this attraction work. Technology has been employed that allows the various computer-animated characters to interact with the audience in real time, meaning that every unscripted show is unique. The often-corny jokes are quite funny, and some are even submitted from audience members via text message. The Magic Kingdom hasn't had a lot of luck with attractions that it has put in this space, but given the technological innovations and interactive nature of the current occupant, that streak should change for the better.

Buzz Lightyear's Space Ranger Spin puts guests into a *Toy Story*–themed shooting game, riding around in "space cruisers" outfitted with laser guns. Riders can spin their cruisers in a full 360-degree rotation, allowing better sighting of the numerous targets. Points are racked up in eight different rooms leading up to a showdown with Buzz's nemesis, Zurg. The super-competitive will want to aim for the diamond- and triangle-shaped targets, as they're worth the most points.

For all the dated retro-futurism of Tomorrowland, it's the noisy exhaust-spewing race cars of the **Tomorrowland Speedway** that actually seem the most anachronistic. Riders are allowed minimal speed-up/slow-down control but can't go faster than 7 mph as the cars meander along their respective rails on the 2,000-foot track. There are always inexplicably long lines for this ride.

Frontierland

If Tomorrowland is all about retro-futurism, then Frontierland is all about retro-retro-ism, evoking a halcyon vision of the Mild West. While one wouldn't expect to see cholera-infested wagon trains or massacres of Native Americans playing a large role in an escapist theme park, the sheer audacious silliness of something like the **Country Bear Jamboree**—in which animatronic bears sing cornpone songs that appeal to the very young and the very old—is something that only Walt Disney could imagine as part of the pioneer experience.

There are thrills to be found in Frontierland, most notably at its two marquee rides. **Big Thunder Mountain Railroad** is a loud and rickety wooden coaster that takes riders on a high-speed run through an abandoned mining town. The careening coaster dips into dark caves and plummets down the mountain, tossing you from side to side as it makes its way along the track. The ride can be quite intense for younger riders.

Splash Mountain is a bit less exhilarating than Big Thunder Mountain, but the 10-minute log flume ride—themed around Br'er Rabbit and his compatriots from *Song of the South*—can be deceptively calming. Multiple climbs and drops happen throughout the ride, and animatronic characters sing songs and tell the story of Br'er Rabbit in a series of densely detailed rooms, but it's the final soaking plunge of nearly five stories that ensures long lines on hot summer days.

Tom Sawyer Island was rethemed in 2007 and is now known as "Pirate's Lair on Tom Sawyer Island." Despite the tie-in to the Johnny Depp film, which resulted in the majority of the island being turned over to things like "The Captain's Treasure" and "Dead Man's Cove," there are still a few elements of the original Twain-inspired attraction like "Tom & Huck's Tree House." Regardless of the facelift, Tom Sawyer Island is one of the least interesting places in the Magic Kingdom; despite a freeform layout that should encourage exploration, the stifling crowds and numerous inaccessible areas make it feel more like a well-decorated ride entrance than an attraction in and of itself.

Food

Ironically, the crown jewel of the Walt Disney World Resort comes up rather short when it comes to dining. While all of the other parks have at least one truly remarkable restaurant option, the Magic Kingdom is notably lacking in this department. The best option is the prix fixe meals at **Cinderella's Royal Table** (breakfast 8 A.M.–10:20 A.M., $31.99 adults, $21.99 children; lunch noon–3 P.M., $33.99 adults, $22.99 children; dinner 4 P.M. until 1 hour before park close, $40.99 adults, $25.99 children). The intimate dining room feels regal, with its high cathedral-like ceilings and windows that give a bird's-eye view of Fantasyland. Breakfast is an all-you-can-eat selection of eggs, bacon, yogurt, fruit, and other morning standards, while lunch and dinner are built around things like pan-seared salmon, roast chicken, grilled pork tenderloin, and more. As this is a character dining location, reservations are pretty much mandatory; dinner includes a souvenir photo package with a shot of you and your party in the lobby. Tableside visits from princesses and free snapshots aside, the menu here is a bit drab and quite overpriced.

There are a couple of other alternatives to the seemingly endless offerings of hamburgers, hot dogs, and turkey legs throughout the Magic Kingdom. The **Liberty Tree Tavern** (hours vary, main courses from $11.99) is a spacious sit-down eatery in Liberty Square that, in keeping with its neighborhood's Early America theme, offers fare ranging from clam chowder and roast turkey to pot roast, along with a few surprises like a vegetarian noodle bowl, "William Penn Chicken Pasta," and a surprisingly healthful kids menu. It's usually pretty easy to get a table.

Tomorrowland Terrace Noodle Station (hours vary, main courses from $6.99) is a counter-service open-air dining option sitting on the boundary of Main Street, U.S.A., and Tomorrowland. Noodle bowls are the centerpiece of the menu, along with a selection of Asian-inspired vegetarian dishes and, uh, chicken nuggets.

Special Events
Mickey's Not-So-Scary Halloween Party (selected dates Sept.–Oct.) and **Mickey's Very Merry Christmas Party** (selected dates Nov.–Dec.) are separately ticketed events that transform the park into a holiday-themed nighttime experience complete with special parades, shows, and fireworks displays; most attractions and rides are operational during these events. Ticket prices change annually but are typically less than a single-day single-park admission ticket.

EPCOT
Divided into two slightly incongruous sections—the technology-driven Future World and the international expositions of the World Showcase—Epcot has taken a while to shake off its early identity crisis as the Disney park that doesn't seem like a Disney park. For much of its early life, visitors would arrive to Epcot expecting amusement-park rides and Mickey Mouse ears, only to be befuddled when confronted with Italian acrobats and the House of Tomorrow. Today, the park stands quite well on its own, with a combination of exciting attractions like Mission: Space and Test Track, interesting semieducational pavilions that easily outclass your favorite science center, and the crash course in global culture that comes from a walk around the "world."

Future World
Half of the "permanent World's Fair" atmosphere of Epcot comes across in the inventions, innovations, and corporate sponsorships that are found throughout Future World. Putting forth a vision of an ecologically balanced, remote-controlled tomorrow, the various pavilions and attractions of Future World combine to create something like the world's biggest hands-on museum that just happens to have some really cool rides.

Spaceship Earth is not one of those cool rides. This is the iconic "giant golf ball," and although it has recently undergone a thorough renovation, the ride inside the ball is far from the most exhilarating experience. Cars slowly make their way along the constantly moving track as animatronic figures and a narration by Judi Dench trace the history of communication from cave paintings and Roman couriers all the way through television and email. Afterwards, riders exit through "Project Tomorrow," an area with interactive games that highlight the technology of current sponsor Siemens.

WALT DISNEY'S VISION OF EPCOT

Walt Disney's original plan for Epcot was for it to be a thriving independent city, built on a progressive platform of New Urbanism and technology-driven efficiency. Disney envisioned a village bustling with more than 20,000 residents who utilized monorails and PeopleMovers like the ones you can still ride in the Magic Kingdom on the Tomorrowland Transit Authority.

This vision was fundamental to Disney's original plans for the Florida Project he began work on in the late 1950s, as Walt had become increasingly distressed by what he saw as the deleterious effects of urban life as well as the anonymous effects of suburban sprawl. The meticulous planning that his staff employed at Disneyland, reasoned Walt, could simply be applied to the creation of a self-contained city. The same way that unsightly but necessary functions were shielded from public view, delivering the uncluttered landscapes and halcyon experiences his amusement park was known for...well, that wouldn't be that hard to translate into a city, would it?

Obviously it was. Even though Walt passionately continued to work on plans for Epcot while on his deathbed, after he died the company's board didn't hesitate to put those plans aside, deeming them too expensive, too impractical, and not in line with the business's main mission: delivering family entertainment.

In the late 1970s the idea was revived as a possibility, though it quickly transformed from a residential community into a sort of permanent World's Fair, with exhibitions of science and technology paving the way for the utopian cityscapes Walt Disney so longed to create. The result was EPCOT Center, now known as Epcot, which opened in 1982. Although very little of Walt's original vision for Epcot is evident in the current park, the best place to see what it might have become is the town of Celebration, about 10 minutes from the main gate of Walt Disney World. Originally owned by the Walt Disney Company, the small village delivered on some of the retro-futuristic promise of Walt's original approach to Epcot – sans PeopleMovers and monorails. The community is mocked by some as a prefab Stepford-type town, but in the eyes of some architects and developers, it's acknowledged as a model of New Urbanism.

Another giant ball at Epcot is the sphere that sits outside of **Mission: Space.** However, that's about the only similarity this ride has to the enervating journey one has on Spaceship Earth. If the many multiple signs and cast-member admonitions warning away the pregnant, heart-troubled, and easily frightened aren't enough of a clue, be advised that Mission: Space is the most intense ride on Disney property. Built on flight-simulator technology, the ride is themed to within an inch of its life as riders are transformed into a crew about to embark on a journey to the red planet. Of course, there is no actual launch, but the perfectly choreographed combination of computer animation, ride environment, and intense g-forces will very nearly fool your mind and body into believing that you've broken the bonds of gravity. In reality, you're just in a rapidly spinning centrifuge with your face plastered up against a tiny movie screen.

The two pavilions that make up the **Innoventions** plaza are stuffed with corporate-presented educational-experimental exhibits like "The Magic of Plastics" (sponsored by the Society of the Plastics Industry), "Where's the Fire?" (sponsored by Liberty Mutual), and the "Great American Farm" (American Farm Bureau). Kids have a chance to interact with several of the exhibits, most notably the "Test the Limits" area, where the folks at Underwriters Laboratories get to show off their various testing techniques.

While Innoventions is one of the less-crowded areas of Epcot, the nearby **Test Track** typically boasts the park's most gruelingly long lines. This ride's FastPass kiosks are typically out of tickets by midday, and during

DIVEQUEST

Although the 5.7-million-gallon aquarium at the Seas pavilion provides plenty of aquatic beauty on the dry side of the thick glass walls, scuba-certified individuals can get even closer to the sharks, fish, and rays by taking part in DiveQuest. The bulk of the three-hour program is a guided backstage tour of the aquarium facilities, but the highlight is a 45-minute dive inside the coral reef habitat as tourists peer at you from the other side of the glass. Although the program is expensive – $175, theme park admission not required – it's quite a remarkable underwater excursion, combining perfectly controlled conditions and the typical Disney service (all dive gear is provided, as well as snacks afterward, and a DVD copy of footage of your dive is available for purchase). Divers must have current open-water adult dive certificates; in the case of kids age 10 and up, Junior Diver Certifications are also accepted. Reservations should be made at least a few days in advance (farther ahead during peak seasons) by calling 407/939-8687.

---

peak season the "standby" line is usually 90 minutes or longer due to frequent instances of the track shutting down for 5 or 10 minutes at a time. Advice: Don't be dissuaded by the crowds; abandon your group and head for the single-riders line, which is usually less than half the length of the standby line. Even if you have to stand in one of the longer lines, Test Track is not to be missed. Sponsored by General Motors, the attraction purports to recreate the various tests that an automobile is put through before making its way to market. Bumpy roads, hot-and-cold temperature extremes, and hair-raising braking tests are the opening acts for a quick 65-mph ride down the steeply banked outdoor track; the last part only lasts for less than a minute, but it's a screaming bit of fun.

It's not exactly clear why the justifiably praised **Soarin'** attraction is in the agrarian-focused pavilion called **The Land,** but regardless of the incongruity of its location, this transplant from Disney's California Adventure in Anaheim has proved to be remarkably popular. Riders board a floorless flight simulator positioned in front of an enormous floor-to-ceiling movie screen. After liftoff, the seats move in tandem with the motion onscreen, realistically emulating the sensation of hang-gliding over various sights in California. While it would have been nice if they had at least made Epcot's version of Soarin' a little Florida-centric, the thrill of fake flight is powerful indeed. Lines for Soarin' are nearly as outrageous as those for Test Track; with that in mind, the indoor line has recently been outfitted with motion-sensitive technology that gives guests an opportunity to play interactive video games on screens overhead.

More appropriate to its location in The Land is, well, **Living with the Land,** a narrated boat ride expounding on various methods of agriculture. Boring? Not so much. The combination of history lesson, ecological message, and the closing coup de grâce—a look at functioning futuristic hydroponic, aeroponic, and aquaculture labs, complete with gigantic gourds and Mickey-shaped cucumbers—proves to be surprisingly interesting. For an extra fee, guests can take the **Behind the Seeds Tour** ($12 adults, $10 children), a 45-minute close-up of Living with the Land's greenhouses.

The Seas with Nemo and Friends used to be a pavilion known as "The Living Seas," but given the success of *Finding Nemo,* the updated theming is a natural fit. The primary attraction here is a ride that is also called "The Seas with Nemo and Friends," an updated version of a more straightforward "sea cab" ride that used to guide visitors through the various features of the aquarium. Now, the sea cabs are "clamobiles," and animated versions of various characters from the film are projected to appear as if they're swimming with the inhabitants of the 5.7-million-gallon aquarium. While seeing Dory and Bruce may be appealing to the younger ones, it's that aquarium—the second-largest manmade saltwater tank in the world—that holds the real stars of the Seas: more than 200 different species, including sharks, turtles, rays, tropical fish, and dolphins. The "Sea Base" area is set up like most public aquariums, and small educational stations are set up throughout. If you've still got questions, a great place to get them answered is **Turtle Talk with Crush,** an animated and interactive show that utilizes the same technology employed at the Magic Kingdom's Monsters, Inc. Laugh Floor; an actor mimics the voice of Crush and responds to audience questions, while the animated turtle moves in real time, as if he can actually see the people in the crowd. It tickles kids to no end, and adults will be fascinated at the Imagineering prowess employed.

Universe of Energy houses a 45-minute show featuring Ellen DeGeneres called "Ellen's Energy Adventure," and the **Imagination Pavilion** has a 3-D movie called "Honey I Shrunk the Audience." Both of these pavilions are easily skipped.

World Showcase

There are 11 countries represented in Epcot's World Showcase. Five are European, three are North American, two are East Asian, and tiny Morocco is left to represent the entirety of Africa and, I guess, the Middle East too. While nobody would attempt to argue that leaving out India and all of South America makes for a remotely representative way to showcase the world, this theme park section is as unique as it is improbable. There are very few actual rides or attractions in this part of Epcot, but the charming tourist-brochure image of each country that is represented makes for a fantastic way to spend an afternoon.

There are rides like Mexico's **Gran Fiesta Tour** (a lazy-river boat ride through various tourist sites; a recent update incorporated a *Three Caballeros*–era Donald Duck while excising some of the more 1980s-specific imagery) and Norway's **Maelstrom** (a dark and briefly exhilarating boat ride that manages to incorporate trolls, Vikings, and oil rigs), but these are the exceptions. Most countries highlight live-action performances like the Beatles tribute band in the UK pavilion, the **Dragon Legend Acrobats** in "China," or the demonstrations by **Miyuki** (who sculpts candy into animal shapes) in the Japan pavilion.

For the most part, the allure of the World Showcase is simply circumnavigating the lake, a pleasant walk that allows one to start in "Mexico" and end in "Canada," taking in food, drink, and tchotchkes from all over "Italy," "Germany," "France," "America," and more in the process. If this sounds like it would be boring for television-addled kids, it's actually not; kids thrive on the wildly varying sights and sounds, and the cast-members in each country take extra care to make their pavilions feel less like a World Cultures lecture and more like an animated adventure. In the interest of real animated adventures and corporate synergy, Disney recently launched the **Kim Possible World Showcase Adventure,** a Showcase-wide scavenger hunt that has kids working on behalf of the cartoon detective to track down the bad guys using something called a "Kimmunicator" and clues found in each pavilion.

Food

Of all the Disney parks, Epcot is the one where, no matter what your culinary inclinations, you should have no problem finding something to eat. The Norwegian-themed **Akershus Royal Banquet Hall** (Norway pavilion) and the fresh-food-peddling **Garden Grill** (The Land pavilion) both offer character dining. The **Coral Reef** restaurant at the Seas pavilion offers fresh seafood, although you'll be surrounded by a saltwater tank and your kids will likely have just finished communing with Nemo, so it may actually be somewhat unsettling.

For quick-service dining, the 🅲 **Sunshine Season** food court is far and away the best option. Located in the Land pavilion, it offers and array of ultra-fresh and veg-friendly dishes ranging from sandwiches, soups, and salads to wok-tossed Asian dishes and noodle bowls as well as rotisserie chicken and salmon cooked over a wood-fired grill.

The best of the nationalistic dining options

EATING AND DRINKING AROUND THE WORLD

A popular pastime at Epcot is to show up with an empty stomach, skip right past the rides and science exhibits of Future World, and eat and drink one's way around the world...or at least around the World Showcase. While this can be fun any time of the year, it's most enjoyable during the annual **Food & Wine Festival,** held late September–early November. In addition to the regular array of treats and tipples the World Showcase offers, the Festival adds dozens of kiosks serving tapas-style nibbles and various beer and wine samples. Most of the regular World Showcase countries are represented with kiosks, but there are also more than a dozen additional countries serving food and drinks; 2009 featured fare from India, Greece, Spain, and several other countries that don't have year-round representation at Epcot. The food samples usually cost $2.50-5, and drinks are typically $5-7.

---

is the exquisite **Bistro de Paris;** reservations are mandatory at this dinner-only establishment, which also enforces a resort-casual dress code. Abstaining from flip-flops is a small sacrifice for the decadent (and expensive) dishes; while not strictly limited to French cuisine, the preparations are elegant and precise. Less intimate but still serving remarkably good food is **Les Chefs de France,** which serves up traditional fare—quiche, crepes, goat cheese salad and more—as well as a macaroni-and-Gruyère casserole that will have you forever foreswearing the blue-and-yellow boxes.

Also recommended would be the modern flair of Japan's **Tokyo Dining** and the **Rose and Crown** in the UK pavilion; the latter's menu options are limited to traditional pub food, but it's prepared excellently and the atmosphere is extra-friendly, even by Disney standards. Don't neglect to pick up a churro and a potent frozen margarita at Mexico's **San Angel Inn** or one of the signature frozen teas at the stand across from the China Pavilion.

Special Events
In addition to the **Food & Wine Festival** (late Sept.–early Nov.), the annual **International Flower & Garden Festival** (spring) draws amateur horticulturists and backyard gardeners for topiary-gawking as well as tips and workshops.

DISNEY'S HOLLYWOOD STUDIOS

Disney's Hollywood Studios didn't exactly get off to a blockbuster start. Opened in 1989 as Disney-MGM Studios, it was the third park to open at Walt Disney World, hastily conceived as a response to the construction of Universal Studios Orlando; when the park opened it only had four attractions. Today, the renamed park houses the two most thrilling attractions on Disney property—Aerosmith's Rock 'n' Roller Coaster and the Twilight Zone Tower of Terror—and the setting combines Hollywood's Golden Age glamour with a sprinkling of Pixar's modern moviemaking magic. Although it's still the lesser of the four parks, it has more than overcome its initial stumbles and now boasts plenty that's worth seeing.

Hollywood Boulevard
Just like the Magic Kingdom's Main Street, U.S.A., Hollywood Studio's Hollywood Boulevard is a mood-setting thoroughfare that allows visitors to slough off the outside world and transport themselves into the glory days of Hollywood. Appropriately, the only real "attraction" here other than an array of shops is **The Great Movie Ride.** One of the original attractions that opened with the park in 1989, this ride is definitely showing its age. Viewers ride on a tram that takes them through a sort of "living" highlight reel of the last 100 years of moviemaking. Extensive set pieces and animatronic figures recreate scenes from *Casablanca, Public Enemy No. 1, Alien,* and more. You may find yourself wishing that your ultra-chatty tour guide would get kidnapped along the

Star Tours combines the Force with the magic of Disney.

way…and your dream will end up coming true. The 20-minute ride culminates with a montage of great film moments, all set to a majestic and heart-tugging score.

Animation Courtyard

Several of the attractions in the Animation Courtyard continue the movie-museum theme of the Great Movie Ride; **The American Film Institute Showcase, Walt Disney: One Man's Dream,** and **Journey Into Narnia: Prince Caspian** are walk-through attractions stuffed with memorabilia and artifacts. Appropriately, One Man's Dream is the best of the three, and though predictably hagiographic, it does give a somewhat comprehensive look at the life of the man behind the mouse. The Narnia exhibit, on the other hand, is little more than an air-conditioned commercial for the movie; as Disney has opted out of future Narnia films, this exhibit is likely to be pulled soon.

The AFI exhibit is really just a small exhibit space at the end of the **Studio Backlot Tour;** the theme of this space changes semiregularly, and you can visit it without going on the Backlot Tour ride. Still, going to Hollywood Studios without going on the Backlot Tour would be like going to Universal without seeing Jaws. Be prepared to commit a good bit of your time to this attraction, as the various walk-through areas, special effects demonstrations, and of course, the tram ride through the Backlot (complete with a very loud and explosive surprise) can take 30–45 minutes.

For the young ones who are less interested in movie magic and more interested in seeing their favorite characters, the **Voyage of the Little Mermaid** and **Playhouse Disney – Live on Stage** are two live action performances. The former is heavily dependent on some impressive special effects, while the latter is driven by audience participation and lots of singing and dancing.

Pixar Place

Formerly an infrequently used and lightly trafficked part of the Animation Courtyard, Pixar Place now houses one of Hollywood Studios' most popular attractions, **Toy Story Mania.** This is a shooting ride, similar to the Buzz

Lightyear ride at Magic Kingdom; however, Toy Story Mania has the added awesomeness of being in 3-D. While certainly not the most original ride concept, the execution of this attraction is flawless, from the heavily themed and interactive queue area where you become "toy-sized" to the impressive 3-D effects.

Backlot

The Backlot area of Hollywood Studios is not, oddly enough, where the Backlot Tour is. Rather, this somewhat haphazard agglomeration of rides and attractions seems more like the area where the park designers said "We've got some cool stuff…now, where do we put it?" Given its location in the back corner of the park, it's actually quite easy to miss most of the Backlot area, especially the expansive **Honey I Shrunk the Kids** playground (which is adjacent to a food court with plenty of seating for grown-ups) and the superlative **Muppet*Vision 3D** attraction. Although Disney's abilities with the production of these 3-D theaters has improved in the years since Muppet*Vision 3D debuted in 1991, none have been able to approach the relaxed combination of smart-aleck humor, slapstick gags, and pie-in-your-face 3-D effects. (And yes, Statler and Waldorf provide plenty of heckling from their box seats.) One of the last productions overseen by Jim Henson, it has all of the charm and wit the Muppets were known for…but in 3-D.

Fans of the *Star Wars* movies may never get the fully-fledged theme park they've long pined for, but until then there's **Star Tours**, a motion-simulator ride produced in collaboration with George Lucas. While the only movie character to make an appearance is C-3PO, the ride still evokes the thrill of flying a StarSpeeder 3000 through a galaxy far, far away. This is another attraction from the early days of the theme park, and it could greatly stand for a refurbishing to take advantage of the 20 years of digital technology that have happened in the meantime. Four Disney parks have a Star Tours attraction, but only Hollywood Studios has the **Star Wars: Jedi Training Academy,** a live-action stage show that allows kids to interact with Chewbacca, Darth Maul, Darth Vader, and other characters from the films.

In keeping with the Backlot theme, there are two movie-themed stunt shows, the **Lights, Motors, Action! Extreme Stunt Show**—which shows off an array of chase-scene and car stunts—and the **Indiana Jones Epic Stunt Spectacular,** which, predictably, re-creates scenes from *Raiders of the Lost Ark*.

Echo Lake

In the central Echo Lake area of the park, visitors can take part in **The American Idol Experience,** which allows guests to register for a daily series of auditions held in front of a live audience; the end-of-the-day winner gets to participate in a real competition for a spot on the television show. Also in this area of the park is **Sounds Dangerous with Drew Carey,** a sound-effects show that happens in total darkness.

Sunset Boulevard

The two marquee attractions at Hollywood Studios are located within yards of each other at the end of Sunset Boulevard, so expect considerable congestion when making your way through the turkey-leg vendors and gift shops along this route. Your persistence will pay off, though, as **The Twilight Zone Tower of Terror** and the Aerosmith-themed **Rock 'n' Roller Coaster** are not just the two best rides at Hollywood Studios, they may be the two best rides on Disney property.

The Tower of Terror puts riders on a ghostly malfunctioning elevator inside the seen-better-days Hollywood Tower Hotel. The theming of this ride is incredibly impressive and detailed down to the last cobweb on the lobby's registration desk. While the *Twilight Zone* references may be lost on some generations of riders, there is a thrill in making your way through the hotel's 13 floors and then dropping like a stone when your elevator malfunctions, only to be jerked back up when it recovers…only to fall again and again; the drops are randomized, so riders never know when and how often they'll plummet.

The Rock 'n' Roller Coaster is an extremely

fast indoor coaster that would be a screaming success even without the presence of aging rockers Aerosmith. The combination of the high-volume soundtrack, the 0-to-60-in-3-seconds launch, and a series of high-speed loops and corkscrews, all in neon-flecked darkness, makes for a chart-topping *(groan)* coaster experience.

For the less thrill-inclined, Sunset Boulevard is also home to **Beauty and the Beast – Live on Stage,** an extravagant stage production that distills the highlights of the animated film into a half-hour cavalcade of live action, songs, and dance.

Food

Disney's Hollywood Studios is home to several excellent restaurants, including the two best in-park dining experiences within the entire resort. (**The Hollywood Brown Derby** (lunch 11:30 A.M.–3 P.M., dinner 3:30–10:30 P.M., main courses from $14) is a little pricey but well worth the expense. Emulating the Golden Age of Hollywood elegance of its namesake, this Brown Derby serves an appropriately classic selection of dishes—strip steak, pork rib chops, grilled salmon—along with more contemporary plates like ahi tuna and a coconut-tofu noodle bowl. And yes, they make a mean Cobb salad here. The atmosphere is upscale but also decidedly relaxed. In comparison to many other in-park restaurants, there's never a sense that you're being rushed to make room for the next wave of diners, and the dining room, though large, is expertly partitioned to create a unique sense of spacious intimacy.

Even more intimate—homey, even—is the (**'50s Prime Time Cafe.** You'll be served by matronly waitresses who admonish diners to finish their veggies and keep their elbows off the table, while an array of black-and-white television sets shows clips from *Father Knows Best, The Donna Reed Show,* and, of course, *The Mickey Mouse Club.* Small dining rooms have Formica tables set out with blue plate specials like fried chicken, meat loaf, pot roast, and an absolutely mind-blowing chicken pot pie. In a not-so-subtle dig at the halcyon imagery of the decade, there's also a full bar adjacent to the dining room, serving everything from classic cocktails and bottled beer to selections from "Dad's Liquor Cabinet."

Special Events

The big seasonal event at Disney's Hollywood Studios is the **Osborne Family Spectacle of Dancing Lights** (Thanksgiving–New Year's). Combining 10 miles of rope lighting, a synchronized musical soundtrack, and 33 snow machines, this holiday display transforms the New York section of the park's Backlot area into a truly impressive winter wonderland.

ESPN: The Weekend (late Feb./early Mar.) finds the Disney-owned sports network broadcasting programs live from the park, along with celebrity athletes on hand to answer questions and sign autographs. **Star Wars Weekends** (late May/early June) caters to an entirely different demographic, as fans of the sci-fi films flock to the park to look at exclusive memorabilia, costumed characters, and the occasional actual star from the films.

Night of Joy (Sept.) is one of two Christian music festivals that happen in Orlando-area theme parks; the other is the Rock the Universe night at Universal Studios, which is usually held on the same dates as Night of Joy. Appropriately, the Disney festival is a little more buttoned-down, focusing less on the sort of alt-rock Christian groups that play at Universal and more on pop-oriented acts.

(ANIMAL KINGDOM

From the moment you pass through the turnstiles at Animal Kingdom, it's clear that this is a different kind of park. There's no expansive entryway with an icon like Cinderella Castle or Spaceship Earth announcing the park's intent; instead, the foliage-draped **Oasis** is a lush maze of animal habitats linked by gently flowing waters and the sounds of chirping birds and splashing mammals. It's a unique mood-setter, preparing you for a park built around ecosensitive concepts and global conservation concerns. It is not—as any Animal Kingdom staffer will tell you—a zoo, but the park is far more focused on observing and learning about animals than it is on delivering thrill rides and character interactions. Sure, you can ride a few great roller coasters here and get your picture taken with Tigger, but the whole Animal Kingdom experience is far more substantial than that, making it not only the newest of all the Disney kingdoms but also the one most worthy of repeat visits.

Discovery Island

Situated in the heart of Animal Kingdom is Discovery Island, which is home to the 14-story **Tree of Life,** an enormous replication of a baobab tree, carved in such a way that images of nearly 400 animals comprise the "bark." The Tree of Life can be seen from throughout the park, but only by getting up close on Discovery Island can you see the intricate work that went into it.

The big attraction in this area of the park is located in the base of the Tree of Life. **It's Tough to Be a Bug** is a 3-D movie experience based on *A Bug's Life,* giving audience members a bug's-eye view of various insects. The 3-D effects are accentuated by seats that rumble and squirt water at unsuspecting viewers. There are a few startles and scares in this experience, so although it's directly targeted at younger crowds, the youngest in your crew may need a few reminders about the difference between movies and reality.

Africa

The Africa section of Animal Kingdom has a little bit of Kenya, a little bit of Zanzibar, a little bit of South Africa, and a little bit of Tanzania. Despite the broad sweep of the pan-African theming, there's a sensitivity and attention to detail in the central "village" of Harambe that's surprisingly effective.

The heart of Animal Kingdom is the **Kilimanjaro Safaris** ride, which puts visitors on a truck that goes out onto the savannas and jungles of the park's expansive animal habitats. There's a story about poachers told by every driver, and a few moments of melodramatic peril, but these bits of acting are entirely superfluous, as the stars of this ride are the dozens of animals one can see on the safari. On busy days the safari ups the number of trucks that run the safari track, so some of the magic can be sapped away while waiting for the vehicles in front of yours to make their way through, but having the chance to get extremely close to giraffes, gazelles, lions, rhinos, and elephants who are just going about their business makes the traffic jams more than manageable.

After disembarking from the safari truck, make your way through the **Pangani Forest Exploration Trail,** a walking trail through a five-acre habitat area filled with meerkats, antelopes, hippopotamuses, and silverback gorillas.

Asia

As ambiguous and all-encompassing as the Africa section the Asia section of Animal Kingdom incorporates Chinese, Indian, Tibetan, Balinese, and Mongolian influences into the fictional kingdom of Anandapur. Just as Asia itself houses more than half of the world's population, you'll sometimes feel as if half of that day's Disney visitors are crammed into the sights and attractions of this part of the park. This is primarily due to the presence of popular rides like the white-water **Kali River Rapids** and the excellent **Expedition Everest** roller coaster. The former is a fairly standard theme-park soaker, accentuated by some environmental messages and some great special effects. As for Expedition Everest, the mere presence of the Abominable Snowman would be enough to make this coaster a winner, but when combined with high speeds, a brief bit of backwards motion, and a 50-foot drop, it's no surprise that this ride is almost always subject to incredibly long lines.

Less adrenaline-pumping is the **Maharajah Jungle Trek,** another expertly themed walking tour through various animal habitats. This one features komodo dragons, tapirs, fruit bats, peacocks, deer, and tigers.

Flights of Wonder is a 25-minute show featuring an array of trained hawks, falcons, parrots, and other birds. The plot of the show is silly and unnecessary, but the birds—and their trainers—are incredibly impressive.

Dinoland U.S.A.

There's a distinct sense of incongruity that you experience when crossing the "Olden Gate Bridge" into Dinoland U.S.A. Part carnival midway—**Chester & Hester's Dino-Rama** features themed-up versions of basic state-fair rides like the **TriceraTop Spin** and **Primeval Whirl**—and part playground (**The Boneyard**), this area of the park is clearly geared toward younger audiences. To that end, there's a live puppetry and dancing show, **Finding Nemo – The Musical,** that's sure to please the elementary school set.

All of this makes the presence of the **Dinosaur** ride something of a horrifying anomaly. After getting the kids all hyped up on the majesty and mystery of dinosaurs, they'll certainly be curious to hop on board this adventure. Bill Nye the Science Guy hosts visitors to the Dino Institute, where he invites them to hop on board a time machine to go back to the time of the giant reptiles. Of course, things go awry, darkness falls, meteors begin raining from the sky, and a giant carnivorous dinosaur begins chasing your vehicle. This ride is loud, dark, and incredibly intense, all of which is great for grown-up thrill seekers. For kids? Not so much. Recently rethemed and, unbelievably, toned down from its original incarnation to incorporate elements of Disney's animated flick of the same name, Dinosaur should be approached with all due caution by those accompanying brontosaurus-loving young children.

Camp Minnie-Mickey

Camp Minnie-Mickey is an excellent place for the kids and grown-ups to fill up their autograph books; the **Camp Minnie-Mickey Greeting Trails** have characters available at regular intervals (check the daily schedule available throughout the park). This area of the park is also home to the popular stage show **Festival of the Lion King.**

Rafiki's Planet Watch

Also known as the "the lines are too long in the rest of the park" area of Animal Kingdom, Rafiki's Planet Watch is well intentioned but pretty inconsequential. Unfortunately, it's also pretty inconvenient. To get here, guests must board the **Wildlife Express Train** for a five-minute ride, only to be greeted by a five-minute walking trail to the actual site. The educational facility offers live animal encounters, a few interactive exhibits, and a peek at the park's behind-the-scenes veterinary work in the **Conservation Station;** there's also the **Affection Section** petting zoo. And yeah, that's it.

Food

The best dining option in Animal Kingdom is Africa's **Tusker House** (open all day, breakfast $18.99 adults, $10.99 children; lunch $19.99 adults, $10.99 children; dinner $26.99 adults, $12.99 children). The buffet-style restaurant hosts a unique breakfast, offering character dining in the form of "Donald's Safari Breakfast." The rest of the day features an incredible selection of pan-global dishes ranging from couscous and vegetable samosas to Cape Malay curry chicken and spiced tandoori tofu, along with more routine plates like grilled salmon, rotisserie chicken, and for the kids, PB and J, mac-and-cheese, and more.

The **Yak & Yeti** restaurant is actually two separate restaurants; guests can take advantage of counter service for simple Chinese dishes like sweet and sour pork and kung pao beef, or they can sit down for a more extensive and expensive menu. Unfortunately, the food here has yet to live up to its location or its prices; despite the beautiful theming of the restaurant, the Chinese fare—glazed roast duck, lo mein, crispy fish, stir-fried beef and broccoli—is nowhere near the quality one would expect for entrées that can range in price from $16.99 to $22.99.

For light bites, head to the **Kusafiri Coffee Shop** inside Tusker House for fresh pastries and coffee, or Asia's **Royal Anandapur Tea Company,** which features a variety of black, green, and oolong teas from around the world.

There is also an outpost of the **Rainforest Cafe** chain at the park's entrance; although the eco-theming is in line with the park's modus operandi, there's nothing spectacular about the menu here other than the eye-popping prices.

Special Attractions

Although Animal Kingdom doesn't host any annual events, it does offer one highly unique experience. The **Backstage Safari** ($70 per person) is a great behind-the-scenes tour that gives guests a peek at the day-to-day maintenance and care of the many animals that live in the park. Also available is the **Wild By Design** tour ($60 per person) that provides insights about the Imagineering that went into the creation of Animal Kingdom.

OTHER DISNEY RESORT ATTRACTIONS

Of course, there's a lot more to this 25,000-acre resort than just the four main kingdoms. Disney's ideal guest is one who arrives on Disney property and doesn't leave until it's time to go home, and to that end, there are dining and shopping areas, hotels, movie theaters, spas, golf courses, and pretty much anything else you would need to occupy your every recreational need for a week or more. The biggest attractions are the two water parks, Blizzard Beach and Typhoon Lagoon, and during the summer they often fill up quite early in the day, forcing staff to prohibit new entries until a requisite number of people have departed. Fear not, though; even if you don't manage to make your way onto the water slides before lunch, there are plenty of other diversions around the resort to hold your attention.

Blizzard Beach

The busier and more thrill-centric of Disney's two water parks, Blizzard Beach ($40 adults, $34 children) is all about breathtakingly high water slides. Sure, the snow-capped theming is amusing, but the focus here is on adventures like **Summit Plummet**, a 120-foot-high beast that propels riders at speeds nearing 60 mph. The **Slush Gusher** gets you going at "only" about 50 mph, and the competitive-minded can race each other on the inner tubes of the **Downhill Double Dipper.** Toboggan mat slides, tube slides, kid-friendly play areas, a lazy river, and a wave pool are also part of the park.

Typhoon Lagoon

Typhoon Lagoon ($40 adults, $34 children) may not offer slides of the same heart-pounding intensity as Blizzard Beach's, but with a water coaster like the impressive **Crush 'n' Gusher** and the 36-foot drop that sliders experience on **Storm Slides,** it's far from sedate. There's also a coral reef environment where guests can snorkel among live sharks and tropical fish, and a surfing-ready wave pool.

ESPN Wide World of Sports

The 220-acre ESPN Wide World of Sports is likely to be of little interest to park visitors who don't have a friend or relative participating in one of the many amateur athletic competitions that take place here. If your visit to Walt Disney World brings you here in March, you can catch the **Atlanta Braves** in spring training; August brings the **Tampa Bay Buccaneers** to the complex for training camp.

Richard Petty Driving Experience

Located somewhat incongruously right next to the Magic Kingdom's parking lots, the Richard Petty Driving Experience allows racing fans to get a shot at riding in—or, if they want to shell out the big bucks, driving—a stock car. There are four different programs, ranging from a one-lap ride-along ($116) that will find you reaching speeds of up to 145 mph to a 30-lap drive around the speedway ($1,385). The driving "experiences" require reservations, and they include a half-hour training session before you get behind the wheel; the ride-along is first-come, first-served. There are no refunds, and weather-cancelled sessions must be rescheduled.

Golf Courses

The Walt Disney World Resort is a prime golfing destination, with five courses, all of which are certified wildlife sanctuaries. All of the 18-hole courses offer GPS-equipped carts;

lessons and club rentals are available at all five courses. **Osprey Ridge** ($154 resort guests, $174 day visitors) is the premier course and was named one of America's Best Resort Courses by *Golfweek* in 2006, and the **Magnolia** course ($154 resort guests, $174 day visitors) is nearly as impressive; the **Palm** and **Lake Buena Vista** courses ($134 resort guests, $154 day visitors) are slightly less expensive (and less challenging), while **Oak Trail** is a nine-hole walking course ($38) for those who want to get a quick round in.

Spas

There are three full-service spas at Walt Disney World, all of which are located in resort hotels. The **Grand Floridian Spa** is as luxurious as its surroundings, while the spa at **Saratoga Springs Resort & Spa** blends that property's old-timey vibe with contemporary massage and spa treatments. The decadent **Mandara** is at the **Dolphin Resort Hotel,** and it is thick with Southeast Asian ambiance; of the three, this is the only one that offers hair and nail services.

Food

Food courts and casual dining options abound throughout the resort. Most are lightly themed to align with the hotel or area in which they reside, and all deliver decent if thoroughly unspectacular food. When you're serving hundreds of thousands of plates a day, it's much more about being efficient than it is about being exceptional.

There are a handful of true destination dining options at the resort, however. They're all a bit pricey, but each is worth it. You'll need to make reservations for most of these restaurants, a process simplified by Disney's automated dining reservation system; just call 407/WDW-DINE (407/939-3463) as far as 180 days in advance. While it's likely that one's schedule—and budget—can accommodate only one or two of these restaurants on a trip to Walt Disney World, any of them are worthy of a foodie's attention.

Jiko – The Cooking Place (Animal Kingdom Lodge, 5:30–10 P.M. daily, main courses $19–39) features an African-inspired menu, accented by Mediterranean and South Asian flavors. Finding quinoa, rocket pesto, figs, curry shrimp, ostrich filet, samosas, and short ribs on one menu may indicate the height of catch-all folly, but an emphasis on strong rustic flavors and rich earthy spices weaves together this broad selection of dishes.

From the moment you step into the LED-lit tunnel that leads you into **The Wave** (Contemporary Resort, breakfast 7:30 A.M.–11 A.M., lunch noon–2 P.M., dinner 5:30–10 P.M., bar area noon–midnight, main courses $8.49–25.99), an atmosphere of stylish modernity is instantly established. This is technically a "casual dining" spot, offering breakfast, lunch, and dinner; although all three meals feature somewhat circumscribed menus, the quiet atmosphere and expert preparation of meat and pasta standards, super-fresh salads, and a daily "sustainable fish" dish make it something of a well-kept secret.

Todd English's Bluezoo (Dolphin Resort, 5–11 P.M. daily, main courses $22–60) serves contemporary American cuisine in a sophisticated and modern environment. Of course, celebrity chef English probably won't be in the kitchen preparing your Cantonese lobster or bacon-wrapped tuna, but the crew on hand does a marvelous job nonetheless. The emphasis here is on fresh seafood—especially fish dishes—but beef, pork, and poultry are also available; vegetarians are likely to find little here that they can eat.

Love great food? Hate crying babies? Head for **Victoria & Albert's** (Grand Floridian Resort & Spa, dinner seatings 5:45–6:30 P.M. and 9–9:45 P.M. daily, six-course prix fixe $125 per person, $185 per person with meal-specific wine pairing). Long the grande dame of Disney dining, Victoria & Albert's not only insists on a dress code (no jeans or capris, much less shorts or flip-flops; jackets are required for men), but recently instituted a rule that requires diners to be at least 10 years of age, the only restaurant in the park to have such a prohibition. While some may fuss over the indignity of not being

THE HOOP-DE-DOO MUSICAL REVUE

Once when I was on assignment for a newspaper I was given the task of reporting back on the Hoop-De-Doo Musical Revue, a long-running pioneer-themed dinner-theater experience at **Disney's Wilderness Lodge**. I had heard that the jokes were corny, the music was corny, and the food consisted of basic plates of fried chicken and corn on the cob. To say the least, I was not excited about the proposition, but reporting back after the fact, I was able to confirm those presumptions: The music and jokes are indeed corny, and dinner is centered around endless plates of fried chicken. But somehow it all works, and if you're capable of shaking off the vestiges of ironic detachment and getting into the spirit of the show, it's an absolute must-do if you'll be on Disney property for more than a few days. The script for the show digs up every hoary joke, pun, and slapstick gag you can imagine and delivers them all in a light-hearted self-aware fashion interspersed with goofy, catchy songs that even the grouchiest attendee will find themselves enjoying. Even teenagers have been known to crack a smile during the show. The food is served in metal buckets that land on your table with a thud, and the chicken, ribs, and other fare is comfort food done right, prepared excellently by a kitchen that could probably get away with doing a lot less.

There are three shows nightly, at 5, 7:15, and 9:30 P.M., and each show lasts about two hours from the time you're seated. There are three seating categories: The most expensive ($59.99 adults, $30.99 children 3-9) gets you a table in the middle area closest to the stage; category 2 ($54.99 adults, $26.99 children 3-9) still provides great seats, although they're a bit further from the stage or in the middle of the balcony; and the "cheap" seats ($50.99 adults, $25.99 children 3-9) have good visibility but are located along the sides of the balcony. The price includes appetizers, all-you-care-to-eat entrées, dessert, and soft drinks; beer and wine are available for an additional charge. Reservations are essential (407/WDW-DINE – 407/939-3463), and guests with special dietary needs are easily accommodated as long as those needs are made known at the time you make the reservation.

able to have their toddler along for a six-course $125 meal, the result is a consistently exquisite restaurant experience. From the accompanying harpist and the complimentary rose for the women at your table to the personalized menus featuring anything from elk and kurobuta pork to duck and prosciutto-wrapped lamb, Victoria & Albert's is classic fine dining. If the prix fixe offerings aren't quite extravagant enough for you, foie gras, caviar, and Kobe beef can be had for an additional charge. Also available for an additional charge (add $40 per person, $50 with wine pairing) is a seat at the chef's table in the kitchen, where the chef offers up various nibbles for you to sample and a maid and butler are on hand to tend to your needs.

Artist Point (Wilderness Lodge, 5:30–10 P.M. daily, main courses $20–42) combines an upscale menu with the rustic ambiance of a classic Pacific Northwest hunting and fishing lodge. The result is a menu of fresh and hearty fish dishes, like the cedar plank–roasted salmon, which is glazed in a pear-ginger reduction and served with a hash of pear and smoked pork belly. Steaks, chops, and pan-seared scallops are also on the menu; vegetarians are restricted to potato-filled pot stickers served with edamame and wilted spinach.

DOWNTOWN DISNEY

The roots of Downtown Disney go all the way back to 1975, when it opened as the small Lake Buena Vista Shopping Village. Over time the village has grown considerably. In 1989 a nightlife area called Pleasure Island was opened (it closed in 2008), and by 1997 the small original shopping mall had expanded into two distinct areas, Downtown Disney's Marketplace and West Side. In addition to marquee spots like Cirque du Soleil's theater, DisneyQuest, and House of Blues, there are dozens of restaurants and shops selling goods both Disney and non-Disney.

◖ Cirque du Soleil – La Nouba

One of the Canadian postmodern circus's three permanent productions, *La Nouba* (6 P.M. and 9 P.M. Tues.–Sat., adults $53–117, children $43–94) is one of the most popular—and priciest—attractions at the Walt Disney World Resort. With a custom-built theater containing more than 1,500 seats—none of which are bad, but some of which are excellent—the eight weekly performances routinely sell out. Conceived as more of a night of theater than an excursion to the circus, the performances, in Cirque du Soleil fashion, are dramatic and story-based. Given its location, *La Nouba* is more family-friendly than some of Cirque's racier productions, but by no means is this show any less dazzling. Acrobats, gymnasts, dancers, and stunt performers display their astounding prowess in a highly choreographed and intricately staged fashion. There's a more explicit "circus" theming to *La Nouba* than with some other Cirque performances, and though younger kids may not grasp some of the symbolism and storyline, they'll doubtlessly be wowed by the strength and skills of the performers and the explosively colorful production.

DisneyQuest

DisneyQuest (10:30 A.M.–midnight daily, $43 adults, $36 children, 25 percent discount for tickets purchased online in advance) is basically a video arcade, but in the hands of Disney designers the concept of an arcade is expanded into that of a "virtual theme park." Visitors can take part in "rides" like the Virtual Jungle Cruise and the dizzying Aladdin's Magic Carpet Ride; a clutch of interactive attractions like the excellent Pirates of the Caribbean—which puts you on a boat in the middle of 3-D pirate battles—are truly remarkable. In the Create Zone, budding Imagineers can create toys, learn about animation, and even design—and virtually ride—their own roller coasters.

There's also a room filled with classic arcade games for those who remember when playing video games required a thick roll of quarters.

Food

Part restaurant, part music venue, part tourist trap, **House of Blues** (11 A.M.–11 P.M. Sun.–Mon., 11 A.M.–midnight Tues.–Wed., 11 A.M.–2 A.M. Thurs.–Sat., main courses $11–28) is something of an attraction in and of itself. Like most of the chain's outlets, the one at Downtown Disney maintains a faux-rustic atmosphere that's meant to convince guests they've stumbled upon some swampy roadhouse where the gumbo's hot and the blues are cool. The whole place runs like a well-oiled machine, and the shrimp po'boys, jambalaya, and fried chicken, though tasty, have considerably less personality than the folk art adorning the walls. On Sunday mornings, however, the restaurant extends its reach into the music hall and serves up a spectacular **Gospel Brunch** (seatings at 10:30 A.M. and 1 P.M., $33.50 adults, $17.25 children, children 2 and under free) with mountainous offerings of grits, fried catfish, mac-and-cheese, roast potatoes, biscuits and gravy, and pretty much any other comfort food you need to shake off Saturday night. The feasting is accompanied by top-notch gospel performances; typically it's a local group, but occasionally the likes of the Blind Boys of Alabama grace the stage.

Bongos (11 A.M.–10:30 P.M. daily, bar until 2 A.M., main courses $8–29) gets quite a bit of attention due to its famous owners, Gloria and Emilio Estefan. The expansive Cuban menu ranges from light plates (media noche, Cuban sandwiches, pan con bistec) to hearty dishes like ropa vieja, pork loin, chicharrones, and more; all are rich and tasty, and some boast surprisingly complex flavor profiles. Service here can occasionally be poor, but once you're seated, the playfully stylish atmosphere, stiff mojitos, and nightly performances by a Desi Arnaz impersonator—yes, really—make for a memorable meal.

Irish food, when crafted solely as an accompaniment to whiskey and beer, can often be something of a nightmare. Accordingly, many "Irish pubs" in the United States—especially those targeted at thirsty tourists—are exceedingly liberal with their drink servings and exceedingly lazy in their kitchens. **Raglan Road** (11 A.M.–11 P.M., bar until 2 A.M., main courses $14–28) is certainly willing to pour you a stiff one or three, but they're going to make sure you've got some exceptional food to go along with 'em. While including all the expected staples—shepherd's pie, bangers 'n' mash, fish-and-chips—Raglan's kitchen also sneaks roasted ham, pork loin, lemon sole, pan-roasted chicken, and a number of other examples of atypical pub fare onto the menu. There's live Irish music—and dancing—nightly.

Shopping

Think you've seen every possible permutation of mouse ears and magic wands in the seemingly endless array of gift shops throughout the Disney theme parks? You haven't. The 50,000-square-foot **World of Disney** (9:30 A.M.–11 P.M. daily) purports to contain the largest selection of Disney merchandise in the world, and it's not hard to believe that claim. You'll find everything from key chains and coffee mugs to luggage, jewelry, and even kitchen goods stuffed into this enormous outlet.

Surprisingly, the majority of the shopping options at Downtown Disney aren't specifically Disney-related. **Magic Masters** has an array of novelties, tricks, and magic guides, and the **LEGO Imagination Center** is part building-block museum and part toy megamart, while the expansive **Virgin Megastore** offers a wide selection of CDs, DVDs, electronics, and vinyl records. Other stores focus on niche items like swimwear (**Summer Sands**), bath soaps (**Basin**), cigars (**Sosa Family Cigars**) and even magnets (**Magnetron**). Most stores in Downtown Disney are open 10 A.M.–10 P.M.

ACCOMMODATIONS

Most visitors to Walt Disney World are faced with the decision of whether or not to stay on Disney property. The rates at most on-site hotels are a bit higher than at nearby places, but there are some distinct advantages to bear in mind. Guests who stay within the resort are entitled to take advantage of the complimentary Disney's Magical Express service, which picks them up from the airport and drops them and their bags at their hotel. Combined with the near-constant availability of bus transportation throughout the resort, guests who arrive intending to only explore Disney property will have all of their transportation needs taken care of, negating the need for a rental car.

Disney hotels are divided into three categories—value, moderate, and deluxe. But regardless of which tier you choose, the basics remain the same: an immaculately clean (if small) guest room located in a large, well-equipped hotel complex filled with swimming pools, dining options, recreational activities, and thousands of other tourists. As one ascends from "value" to "deluxe," the amenities and atmosphere scale accordingly, but even the most basic level of service on Disney property is in line with the best midrange national chain hotel.

Resort Hotels

For on-site reservations, call 407/939-7429.

One of Walt Disney World's four "value" resorts, the **Pop Century Resort** (near Wide World of Sports; from $115 d) is the newest and the most fun. Ten blindingly bright motel-style buildings are painted in decade-specific themes, and the property is festooned with enormous renditions of pop-culture artifacts like yo-yos and Rubik's cubes. The buildings house an eye-popping 2,880 guest rooms, and accordingly the queues in the enormous food court and the crowds in any of the three pools can sometimes be daunting.

The "moderate" resorts (from $185 d) are best represented by the **Coronado Springs Resort** and the **Port Orleans French Quarter Resort.** Coronado Springs is large but charming and well-organized, with 1,900 guest rooms divided among "casita," "rancho," and "cabana" buildings, all of which are easily accessible from the main registration-dining-pool areas. The French Quarter resort has "only"

The Swan hotel is one of Disney's most luxurious properties.

1,000 guest rooms but is laid out in a fashion that's very nearly quaint, with wrought iron fences and beautiful landscaping. It shouldn't be confused with the similarly named **Port Orleans Riverside Resort;** that one was formerly known as Dixie Landings, and its 2,000 guest rooms are spread out on property enormous enough to be nearly unnavigable. All of the guest rooms in the moderate resorts are around 325 square feet.

Somewhat surprisingly, the majority of Disney's on-site accommodation options fall into their "deluxe" category, but again it's worth noting that the primary difference between these big-ticket guest rooms and their less-expensive counterparts is primarily one of atmosphere and amenities; beds are comfortable and guest rooms are clean throughout the entire resort, so if you're just looking for a pillow to rest your park-wearied head on, there's little reason to splurge on these deluxe guest rooms.

However, those who do indulge themselves will find the splurge memorable. **Animal Kingdom Lodge** (from $290 d) is themed to emulate the experience of staying at a safari lodge. Employing lots of dark wood, natural light, and African craftwork, the ambiance is intensely evocative. Guest rooms are comfortably appointed, and a full-service spa, deluxe lounge, and enormous pool area add to the elegance. What's outside the back door truly sets this resort apart; the planners devised a way to recreate an African savanna—complete with wild-roaming zebras, gazelles, giraffes, and other animals. A recent addition to the property is the **Jambo House** (studios from $389, one-bedroom villas from $530, two-bedroom villas from $970), a collection of 216 villa-style accommodations that shares the amenities of the lodge but with larger units designed for extended stays.

The **Walt Disney World Swan and Dolphin Resort** (from $300 d) is actually two hotels, the "Swan" and the "Dolphin," logically enough. Operated by Starwood Hotels and typically catering to well-heeled conventioneers and high-end travelers, the resort is stylish and modern. Boasting one of Disney's signature restaurants—Todd English's Bluezoo—as well as a Shula's Steak House, a Japanese restaurant (Kimono's, which also features a lively, after-hours karaoke scene), and the requisite activities needed to burn those calories off (a spa, health club, tennis courts, swimming pools), the Swan and Dolphin's level of luxury is almost high enough to make one consider forgoing rollercoasters and character visits for a day. The resort is located near Epcot, and, like all Disney accommodations, is serviced by Disney buses; an added bonus, though, is the boat service you can take directly into a secluded entrance into Epcot near the World Showcase.

For a truly upscale experience, the most well-heeled guests head for the **Grand Floridian Resort & Spa** (from $529 d). From the stained-glass windows adorning the soaring atrium lobby and the enormous chandeliers to the spacious guest rooms, the Grand Floridian exudes Victorian elegance throughout its six buildings. Views across the Seven Seas Lagoon to the Magic Kingdom only add to the charm. The resort is also home to

Disney's best restaurant, Victoria & Albert's, and an award-winning spa.

Though technically one of Walt Disney World's "moderate" offerings, (**The Cabins at Disney's Fort Wilderness Resort** ($355) are a truly unique lodging experience, and are strongly recommended for those traveling with children or those planning an extended stay. The 500-square-foot buildings won't be mistaken for mansions, but the idea of having a home away from home in your own free-standing building is certainly appealing. Spread throughout the campground are 409 cabins, and each has one bedroom with a bunk bed and a double bed, along with a Murphy bed in the living room; truly economical travelers can take advantage of the full kitchen and charcoal grill to prepare their own meals. The DIY ethos, thankfully, does not extend to toilet-scrubbing and bed-making, as each cabin is serviced daily by the resort's housekeeping crew. Fort Wilderness is somewhat remote, which is a blessing when one wants to escape the crowds, but it also means you'll experience somewhat longer travel times when going to and from the parks.

Nearby Hotels

Buena Vista Suites (8203 World Center Dr., 407/239-8588, two-room suites from $129) and **Caribe Royale** (8101 World Center, 407/238-8000, www.cariberoyale.com, from $209 d) are adjacent to one another about a mile from Walt Disney World, and both are highly recommended. The 279 two-room suites at Buena Vista recently underwent a massive stem-to-stern renovation, and the result is a stylish and comfortable hotel with amenities like flat-screen HDTVs and granite countertops. More importantly, the affordable guest rooms are sparklingly fresh. Caribe Royale has more of a resort–convention center vibe, with a massive pool area and an endless array of meeting rooms tucked down its labyrinthine hallways. One-bedroom suites have microwave-fridge combos, while the two-bedroom villas are equipped with full kitchens.

If your theme-park visit is solely in the service of some television-addled children, **Nickelodeon Family Suites** (14500 Continental Gateway, 866/297-7402, one-bedroom suites from $209) may be just the character-driven destination you need. An extensively redecorated version of a Holiday Inn "KidSuites" facility, the hotel is done up with characters from Nickelodeon cartoons. One-, two-, and three-bedroom suites are decked out with bunk beds, kitchens, and *lots* of primary colors, and the young ones can endlessly occupy themselves in the enormous pool areas, game room, mini-golf area, and even a kids' spa. And yes, for the adults, there is a bar.

For something a little more elegant, the enormous **Gaylord Palms Resort and Spa** (6000 W. Osceola Pkwy., 407/586-2000, from $209 d) is an upscale facility geared more toward conventioneers and business travelers. One of the two pool areas is adults-only, and the recreation area is focused on croquet and a putting green rather than on merry-go-rounds and sandboxes. Families are clearly still welcome here—the other pool area is a raucous one, as screaming kids hurtle down the water slide—but there's a decidedly more adult feel than at any of the nearby resorts.

A bit farther away from Walt Disney World's main entrance is the **Perri House Bed & Breakfast** (10417 Vista Oaks Court, 800/780-4830, from $89 d), an eight-room inn that prides itself on its quiet residential atmosphere. All guest rooms have private baths and their own entrances.

DINING NEAR THE RESORT
Breakfast

Chain diners abound near the park entrance, so finding a plate of eggs and pancakes is never much of a challenge. But for a sumptuous early morning meal, the Sunday champagne brunch at the Hyatt Regency Grand Cypress's **La Coquina** (1 Grand Cypress Blvd., 407/239-1234, 10:30 A.M.–2 P.M., $63.95) is a truly indulgent experience. Only offered seasonally (late Sept.–early June), the meal is a pricey and decadent way to start the day; there is so much food on offer that much of the preparation commences days beforehand, a fact that guests learn as they are given a tour—yes, a tour—of the multitude of cheeses, pastries, fruit, seafood, salads, and desserts that await them. Reservations are essential, and there is a dress code.

Steak and Seafood
Johnnie's Hideaway (12551 State Rd. 535, 407/827-1111, 5–11 P.M. daily, main courses from $14) is located in a ticky-tacky tourist zone directly across from one of Disney's main entrances, but somehow the restaurant manages a relaxed sophistication that proves a welcome respite from the surrounding area. Steaks are dry-aged on-site and are the big draw, but a good selection of fresh seafood, including a raw bar, and Floribbean fare make for a well-rounded menu.

Similarly, ◖ **The Venetian Room** (8101 World Center Dr., 407/238-8060, 6–10 P.M. Tues.–Sat., main courses from $22) defies its location in the bowels of the Caribe Royale resort. Dark-wood furnishings and private dining alcoves make for a tremendously romantic atmosphere that's accentuated by white-glove service. The traditional epicurean fare—filet mignon, bouillabaisse, duck confit, lobster—is appropriate to the classic and classy atmosphere. Be advised that there is a dress code, and reservations are suggested.

International
Across the street from a Disney entrance and next door to a TGI Friday's, ◖ **Dakshin** (12541 State Rd. 535, 407/827-9080, lunch 11:30 A.M.–2 P.M. Sun.–Fri., dinner 5:30–10:30 P.M. daily, main courses from $16) could probably easily get by on serving biryanis and chicken tikka to the throngs of tourists who want to try some Indian food on vacation. Instead, the restaurant specializes in south Indian cuisine—lots of seafood and Kerala-style spices—and presents it in an upscale environment decorated in brass, thick-carved wood, and elegant Indian art. A Kottayam fish curry is a menu highlight, as are the many different dosai that are available. Service can sometimes be slow, but the staff is friendly and the food is well worth both the wait and the price.

INFORMATION AND SERVICES
The one thing you'll never find lacking on Disney property is a smiling face ready to cheerfully answer whatever question you may have. Disney staff members are famously indoctrinated into a sort of cult of customer service, so anyone from the guy sweeping up in Tomorrowland and the ice-cream vendor at the Magic Kingdom to the manager of a gift shop is ready, willing, and able to point you to whatever and wherever you need, and if they can't, they'll be quick to find you someone who can.

Guide maps can be found throughout the parks at nearly every gift shop or concessionaire, and they contain the day's schedule of shows and character meet-and-greets. Dining reservations can be made from any restaurant (even if it's not for that restaurant) or by calling 407/WDW-DINE (407/939-3463).

Strollers and wheelchairs can be rented at any of the kingdoms, and baby feeding and changing stations are located near the entrance of each park.

Animals, with the exception of service dogs, are not permitted in any of the parks, hotels, or other public areas, but there are kennels near the entrance of each park as well as at Fort Wilderness Resort & Campground.

Disney's website (http://disneyworld.disney.go.com) has reams of information about each park and the various other attractions within the resort, including restaurants and shopping opportunities; alternately, there is a guest information line—407/939-6244, 9 A.M.–10 P.M. daily—where customer service staff are available to answer your questions.

GETTING THERE
By Air
There are two airports that serve the greater Orlando area, **Orlando International Airport** (MCO, One Airport Blvd., Orlando,

407/825-2001, www.orlandoairports.net) and **Orlando-Sanford International Airport** (SFB, 1200 Red Cleveland Blvd., Sanford, 407/585-4000, www.orlandosanfordairport.com). The former is one of the busiest airports in the United States and is served by many major American and international carriers. The airport in Sanford is used primarily for charter flights, although one low-cost carrier, Allegiant Air, has regularly scheduled year-round service from several U.S. destinations; additionally, Icelandair as well as Scottish low-cost carrier Flyglobespan offer a few international options.

Since most visitors to the parks arrive via Orlando International Airport, Disney recently introduced **Disney's Magical Express** at the airport, a program that provides complimentary bus transportation from the airport for guests staying at selected Disney resort hotels. It's incredibly convenient door-to-door service (they even take care of your luggage), especially if your visit to Orlando is going to be spent solely at Disney parks. Reservations for Disney's Magical Express must be made prior to arrival, typically when the hotel reservation is made.

By Car

One of the reasons Walt Disney chose Orlando for the site of this resort was the opening of I-4, which connects Tampa (and I-75) on the west coast to Daytona Beach (and I-95) on the east coast; Orlando is right in the middle of the I-4 corridor, making it easily accessible via interstate. The resort is located approximately 15 miles southwest of downtown Orlando and is accessed via five I-4 exits. All of these exits are well marked, giving appropriate guidance depending on which part of the park you're headed for. If you're arriving and heading for a hotel rather than a park, aim for the park that your hotel is associated with and follow the directions rather than your instincts.

GETTING AROUND

Parking at Disney parks is exorbitantly priced; it's currently $12 per car per day, although you are able to use your parking pass in multiple lots throughout the day, and parking is free at Downtown Disney and the water parks. Add to that cost the fact that the lots are enormous, requiring trams to transport guests from the parking area to the main entrance, and using your car to get around the resort becomes a less-than-optimal solution.

I strongly advise the use of Disney's intraresort bus system instead. For guests staying at Disney hotels, this is something of a no-brainer, as each hotel has its own bus stop with regular arrivals and departures. But even for day visitors it's an appealing option, as you can park your car once in the morning and use the buses to move between almost any two locations within the resort easily. The buses are free, and more importantly, they're frigidly air-conditioned.

Universal Orlando Resort

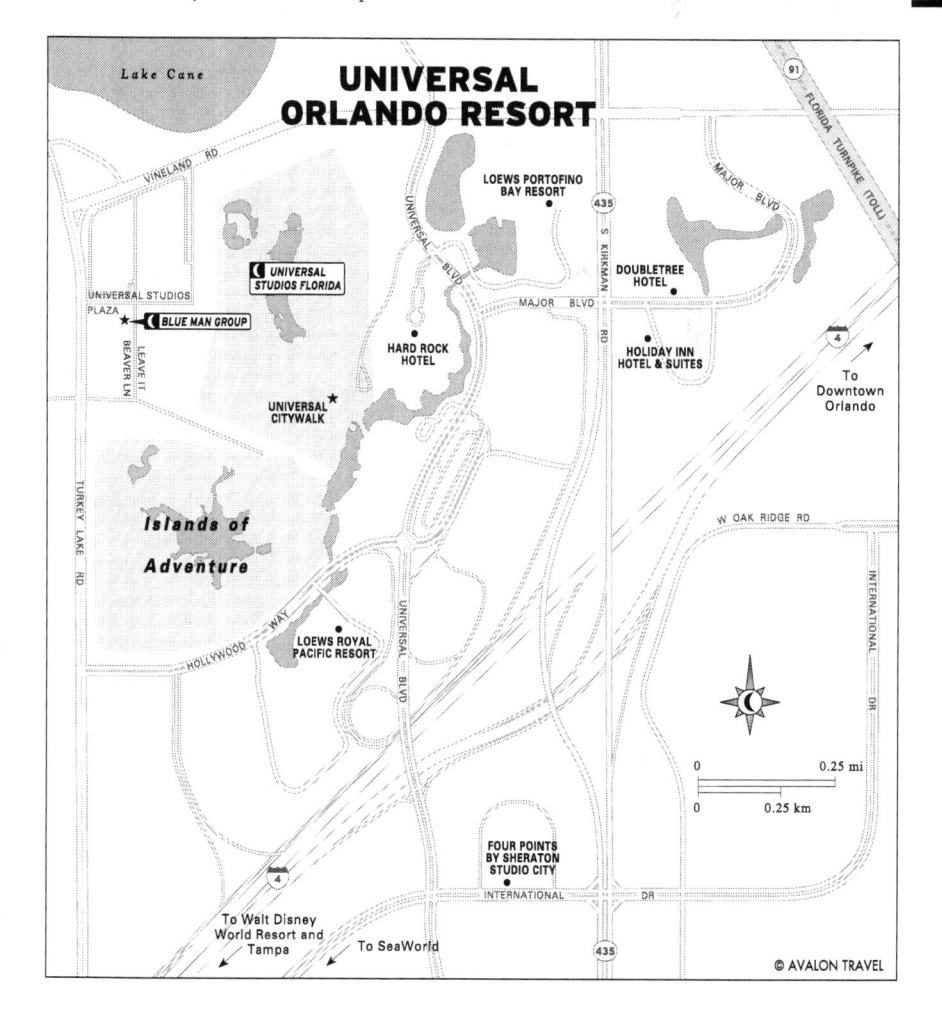

Tours of Universal Studios in Hollywood have been popular since the studio opened, and when those back-lot peeks turned into a full-fledged theme park in the mid-1960s, Universal became the undisputed king of combining amusement-park attractions with movie-making glamour. It was only a decade after the Walt Disney World Resort opened that Universal began making plans to open a theme park in the Orlando area, and those plans came to fruition with the opening of the Universal Studios theme park in 1990. The original park was much more in line with the movie-magic concept of Universal Studios Hollywood, but the addition of Islands of Adventure in 1999—which focused more on thrill rides—has made the Universal Orlando Resort not just a formidable competitor to Disney but also a thematic complement. While Disney's image is all about halcyon Americana and the magic of imagination, Universal pointedly exhibits a bit of a rebellious (read: teenager) streak, stressing its adrenaline-rush coasters and superhero fantasias. As such, you won't find quite the same level of service or fastidiousness at Universal as you do at Disney, and in the shadow of the Mouse, Universal feels like nothing more than a couple of truly exceptional amusement parks. However, taken on their own merits, they easily outstrip every other non-Disney theme park in the country in terms of heart-pumping action and immersive imagination.

One-day one-park admission at Universal Orlando is $73, a price that's in line with admission prices at the Walt Disney World Resort. Getting a deal here requires far less commitment than at Disney: You can add a second park to a one-day pass for an additional $12, or get a two-day two-park pass for $95. Even better: the two-park seven-day pass, which allows unlimited admission to both parks for a week for only $100. Florida residents can get additional discounts, and annual passes are also quite a bargain.

Universal also sells "Orlando FlexTicket" packages, which provide unlimited admission for two weeks to both Universal parks, SeaWorld, Aquatica, and Wet 'n' Wild for $235 adults and $215 children. For an additional $45 you can add Busch Gardens Tampa to the list, and they'll provide round-trip shuttle transportation at no extra cost.

UNIVERSAL STUDIOS FLORIDA

From its opening date in 1990, the theme at Universal Studios Florida has been an exhortation for guests to "ride the movies." That film-centric mission has since been expanded to include television shows, but the basic idea remains the same: This is the park where you go to see Hollywood come to life. There are actual production facilities on-site (although they're not open to the public), but the various

Hollywood Boulevard at Universal Studios Florida

areas of the park are all designed to resemble either soundstages, back lots, or movie scenes come to life. While it doesn't quite capture the Hollywood action of its West Coast predecessor, there's a much more consistent cinematic theming to this park than at Disney's Hollywood Studios.

Hollywood

Designed by director James Cameron, **Terminator 2: 3-D** is a fantastic attraction. Utilizing both live action and 3-D film work (not to mention the thespian abilities of *T2* stars Arnold Schwarzenegger, Linda Hamilton, and Edward Furlong), it's an incredibly immersive and often quite scary attraction, which is an impressive feat considering that there's no actual "ride"—guests are visiting the Cyberdyne plant on a tour, and as the action unfolds around them, it can be easy to forget that it's all make-believe.

The **Universal Horror Make-Up Show** is, well, a scripted show about the use of makeup in horror movies, so it shouldn't be too surprising that it's kind of gross; it's also got a few interactive elements and is pretty funny.

In contrast, **Lucy – A Tribute** manages to reduce one of television's all-time great comediennes to a collection of context-free artifacts.

Production Central

Shrek 4-D puts guests into a theater equipped with buzzing, bumping, and squirting seats to watch an amazingly effective—and pretty hilarious—film featuring Mike Myers, Eddie Murphy, and many of the other voice stars from the *Shrek* films. The 3-D effects are impressive, and the physical gags the theater imposes on guests are a hoot, but what makes the attraction a winner is the smart-aleck humor from the characters.

Jimmy Neutron's Nicktoon Blast is a silly motion-simulator ride that puts you in the middle of the titular cartoon character's science experiments—which, of course, go completely awry. As you "fly" out of the park and into the Nickelodeon universe, characters from other Nickelodeon shows like *SpongeBob SquarePants* and the *Fairly OddParents* take part in the shenanigans.

New York

Universal Orlando made up for its complete lack of roller coasters with the recent addition of **Revenge of the Mummy**, a bracingly fast (45 mph) indoor steel coaster that would be thrilling even without the effective scary Egyptian curse theme. Dark and intense, the ride also features a particularly frightening finale.

Twister...Ride It Out is less a ride than a special effects display, with guests standing on a platform watching wind blow, water spray, and plastic cows fly by. Yes, it's exactly as much fun as that sounds.

San Francisco/Amity

Disaster is little more than a rethemed update of the park's long-standing Earthquake ride. Using a new script and the inimitable presence of a Christopher Walken hologram, the basic premise is the same: Riders on a San Francisco subway train wind up trapped in the middle of various simulated disasters. The effects are still impressive, from the sheets of fire and dousing rain to the rumbling tracks, except now they're part of an in-progress film, making it a bit more interactive than its predecessor and less dependent upon a 30-year-old film for its story line.

Long the signature element of the back-lot tour at Universal Studios in Hollywood, the **Jaws** attraction at the Orlando park expands that singular moment into a full-blown ride. Guests take a ride on one of "Captain Jake's Amity Boat Tours" with the purported intent of gawking at the sites made famous by the movie. Of course, this bit of metaentertainment is interrupted by...well, you know. In addition to the sight of the gaping maw of a giant shark, guests are also treated to an array of explosions and other pyrotechnics.

World Expo

Men In Black Alien Attack has one of the best-themed queue areas of any attraction at Universal Studios. Designed around the conceit that visitors are coming to check out "The Universe & You" exhibition at the 1964 World Expo, the Disney-esque preshow abruptly segues into the "reality" that guests are taking part in a training exercise to become MIB agents. Peeks into labs and coffee-break rooms are funny, helping pass the time until you board your training vehicle. Once on board, the object is to shoot as many aliens as you can with your laser gun; some, however, shoot back, causing your car to spin in rapid circles. Just like in the film, the aliens are often disguised, posing a greater challenge than one might expect.

The arrival of **The Simpsons Ride** at Universal Studios was greeted with mixed emotions by many parkgoers; while many were upset to see the Back to the Future motion-simulator film ride disappear, the idea of a ride themed after the popular animated television series was quite promising. Thankfully, the Simpsons Ride is largely based on the same technology and ride concept as Back to the Future, except instead of hurtling through time with Doc Brown, riders are in Krustyland with the Simpsons family, trying to escape the sabotage efforts of Sideshow Bob. With the addition of 3-D effects and, it must be said, some rather cheesy computer animation, the motion effects of the Back to the Future ride are amplified, and the comedy factor is considerably improved.

KidZone

The preschool and elementary set will find plenty worthy of their attention in the KidZone area, although those without young ones will likely only be drawn here by **E. T. Adventure,** which puts riders on a bicycle "flight" through the world of the movie and onward to E. T.'s home planet, which is apparently populated solely by babies. Nearby, **Woody Woodpecker's Nuthouse Coaster** is a quick, unchallenging coaster with only two mild drops. Other kid-centric attractions here are **A Day in the Park with Barney** (which can be used to threaten your recalcitrant teenager) and two playgrounds: **Curious George Goes to Town** and **Fievel's Playland.**

Food

Beyond the standard array of popcorn stands and hamburger slingers, dining options at Universal Studios are quite limited. Nonetheless, **Finnegan's Bar & Grill** (New York, lunch and dinner daily, main courses from $11) has Irish fare and a warm atmosphere that's surprisingly conducive to leisurely liquid lunches. It's even got daily happy-hour specials. Nearby, **Lombard's Seafood Grille** (San Francisco/Amity, lunch and dinner daily, main courses from $11) is another decent spot for a sit-down meal, with excellent fish and seafood platters. For a great selection of breakfast pastries, **Beverly Hills Boulangerie** (Hollywood, open all day) is very close to the park entrance and provides the calories and caffeine you'll need to prepare for the day; they also serve sandwiches and desserts throughout the day.

Special Events

Universal's annual **Mardi Gras** (Feb.–Apr., $45.95) celebration brings a weekly live concert to the park, usually featuring a cavalcade of '70s and '80s pop stars with a smattering of current hit-makers, as well as a bead-throwing New Orleans–style parade at the end of the evening. Purchase of a Mardi Gras ticket allows you entrance to the park after 5 P.M. and admission to some of the cover-charging clubs of Citywalk after the park closes.

In the fall, the Christian-music-themed **Rock the Universe** (Sept.) festival happens, often on the same day as Disney's Night of Joy concerts. The musicians at Universal's concerts are typically more the alternative and punk bent, while those at Disney's are more pop-oriented.

During the Christmas season, the big event at Universal Studios is the daily **Macy's Holiday Parade,** but there are also Christmas-themed shows throughout the park.

ISLANDS OF ADVENTURE

More focused on rides and coasters than its next-door neighbor, Islands of Adventure is the most thrill-oriented park in Orlando. Although several of the rides have movie

HALLOWEEN HORROR NIGHTS

In 1991, Universal Studios Florida opened the temporary Dungeon of Terror haunted house as a way to drum up nighttime business during a traditionally slow part of the year. That lone haunted house in the queue area for the Jaws ride has since expanded to become one of the premier Halloween-themed events in the country, with nearly 20 haunted houses and "scare zones" transforming one of the two parks into a terrifying themed adventure. Costumed actors roam the fog-covered property, and visitors are never quite sure if that dark corner is hiding a blood-soaked character ready to chase them with a chainsaw. The houses and scare zones fully utilize the set-building and scene-setting prowess of Universal's creative team, so don't show up expecting the same sort of low-rent startles and screams you're treated to at your local haunted house.

The nature of Halloween Horror Nights makes it a decidedly adult affair, and in addition to the shrieks and scares, a lot of folks show up for the festive atmosphere and the copiously available grown-up beverages. Although some parents bring younger children, it's definitely not advised; even if the ax murderers and serial killers don't give them nightmares, which they most certainly will, the occasionally inappropriate behavior of some park guests may leave their ears and eyes burning. This event is incredibly popular, so the park gets very crowded very quickly. It's best to check it out on a weekday evening, but even those crowds manage to be quite large.

Halloween Horror Nights runs early September-November 1 and requires a separate additional admission charge (in 2009 it was $69.99). No costumes or masks are allowed.

---

themes, the park is far more unified by the adrenaline rushes to be had in each of its "islands." There are currently five islands, organized and themed in a fashion similar to the various "lands" at Disney's Magic Kingdom; a sixth island will be solely devoted to the "Wizarding World of Harry Potter," scheduled to open early in 2010.

Marvel Super Hero Island

I hate to accuse the designers of a multimillion-dollar theme park of lack of foresight, but it's truly perplexing that the two best rides on the entire property are not just in close proximity to one another but are also among the first attractions you encounter in the park. To be sure, after experiencing the high-speed **Incredible Hulk Coaster** and the immersive 3-D simulations of **The Amazing Adventures of Spider-Man,** there's little question that Islands of Adventure is exponentially more thrill-focused than its next-door neighbor; unfortunately, the rest of the park has trouble living up to the high standard set by such an introduction.

The two-minute Hulk coaster blasts riders out the launch area at 40 mph, and by the time the steel tracks have you hurtling through an underground tunnel from 100-foot heights, your speed has reached almost 70 mph. Two enormous loops and corkscrews ensure the ride never loses your full attention.

The Spider-Man attraction is equally engaging, as riders are sent out onto the villain-thick streets of New York, recruited by the cigar-chomping publisher of the *Daily Bugle* to get the story in high-tech "Scoop" vehicles. A combination of 3-D film effects, enormous set pieces, and fire and water effects make for a surprisingly visceral and believable ride that culminates in a heart-stopping "fall" from atop a skyscraper.

Other attractions in this area of the park include the X-Men-themed **Storm Force Accelatron,** which is little more than a superhero-soundtracked version of the teacup rides found at state fairs—and Disney parks—everywhere. Likewise, **Doctor Doom's Fearfall** is an uninventive freefall drop ride that propels riders up a 200-foot tower and then drops them…twice.

Toon Lagoon

"Lagoon" is an appropriate place name for this part of the park, as riders of either of its two marquee attractions are bound to get wet. Although many younger visitors are probably unfamiliar with much of the comic-strip theming (does anyone read *Krazy Kat* anymore?), the thrill of the splashing, soaking **Popeye and Bluto's Bilge-Rat Barges** river raft ride is pretty universal. And although the Bullwinkle cartoons that introduced previous generations to the uptight Canadian Mountie are no longer aired, **Dudley Do-Right's Ripsaw Falls** manages to update the idea of the log flume into a surprisingly heart-racing—and butt-soaking—thrill.

Jurassic Park

The theming of the Jurassic Park area of Islands of Adventure is pretty integral to the enjoyment of the premier attraction: **Jurassic Park River Adventure.** If you squint your eyes and take in this flume ride along with the nearby chairlift ride (**Pteranadon Flyers**), the **Camp Jurassic** playground, and the quasi-educational **Jurassic Park Discovery Center,** you can almost imagine that Jurassic Park is its own stand-alone amusement park. And, of course, that park is the same one in the book and films where things went horribly awry. Accordingly, the Jurassic Park River Adventure starts out as informative and relaxing and soon devolves into a pretty tense—and very wet—escape from some pretty scary dinosaurs.

The Lost Continent

Dueling Dragons is the only inverted roller coaster in the world in which riders find themselves—and their feet—coming frightfully close to riders running on another "dueling" track. The "Fire" and "Ice" tracks each have their own proponents, and you'll hear each side arguing their respective merits when it comes time to decide which coaster's queue to enter, though it must be said that the Fire coaster gets up to 60 mph while Ice "only" reaches 55. Regardless of which coaster is chosen, the combination of inversions, loops, corkscrews, and rolls—not to mention the three occasions when the coasters come within a foot of one another—makes Dueling Dragons one of the top attractions at Islands of Adventure.

Poseidon's Fury is a walk-through attraction that combines live action and some stunning special effects; the dark passages, frequent scares, and the impact of the intense climax may be a bit much for younger visitors, but the occasional corny laugh lines delivered by your guide help to ease the tension.

Stunt-show fans may be interested in **The Eighth Voyage of Sindbad,** but most other park guests take their seat in the theater just to get off their feet for a mildly entertaining half hour.

Seuss Landing

All theme parks have an area dedicated to small children, but IOA's Seuss Landing is by far the most charming. The whimsical nature of the classic books elevates standard attractions like the **Seuss Trolley Train Ride,** the **Caro-Seuss-el,** and **One Fish, Two Fish, Red Fish, Blue Fish** (a Dumbo-like ride on which riders control the up and down motion of their vehicles as they spin around) into something altogether more engaging. **The Cat in the Hat** is a must-ride attraction for kids, parents, and even kid-free adults; the dark storytelling ride puts you right into the middle of the classic tale and is filled with spins, careening near-misses, and a sense of sly fun.

Food

While no sandwich at **Blondie's** (Toon Lagoon, lunch and dinner daily, main courses from $7) quite comes close to the enormous ones devoured by Dagwood in the classic comic strip, it's a pleasure being able to get a fresh deli snack instead of the standard burgers-and-fries available throughout the rest of the park.

Diners seeking a somewhat more sophisticated theme-park repast should head straight for **Mythos** (The Lost Continent, lunch daily, dinner daily summer and Christmas). Fresh ingredients and thoughtful preparation are key here, and the menu—though generally leaning

The quirky and youthful spirit of Dr. Seuss is prevalent throughout Seuss Landing.

toward Italian and contemporary fusion cuisines—changes frequently. All of it is accented by some stunning interior design, making for an exceptional dining experience. Accordingly, a meal for two, including wine, can often top the $100 mark, but hey, you're on vacation, right?

Special Events

Holiday festivities are somewhat limited at IOA, but when you've got the most famous holiday curmudgeon on hand, what else do you need? **Grinchmas** is centered around daily performances of *How the Grinch Stole Christmas*, but the real star of the show is the Grinch himself; kids and adults can get their picture taken with him throughout the day.

UNIVERSAL CITYWALK

The CityWalk concept was first explored at Universal's park in Los Angeles, which opened in 1993; when Universal Orlando expanded in 1999 with the opening of Islands of Adventure, CityWalk Orlando was part of that expansion. The entertainment and dining area is not dissimilar to Downtown Disney, though there's far less emphasis here on Universal-themed places and products and a much larger contingent of known national chains. Local teenagers flock to CityWalk on the weekends to take advantage of the spacious 20-screen movie theater and the adjacent eateries, while adults flock to the several nightclubs and music venues.

◖ Blue Man Group

Built, as so many things at Universal Orlando are, in response to a success at Disney (in this case, Downtown Disney's Cirque du Soleil theater), the purpose-built Sharp Aquos Theater hosts daily performances of the Blue Man Group (showtimes vary, daily, adults $64–84, children $54–74, children 2 and under free, but not recommended for children under 3). The Orlando production is one of seven permanent Blue Man productions, and the show here is something of a "greatest hits," incorporating various elements from different Blue Man shows. The oddball instrumentation, choreographed feats, physical humor, and general sense of amazement that the Blue Men are known for are amplified in the intimate theater setting, and the 100-minute show is both hilarious and impressive.

Clubs and Bars

While Downtown Disney has largely given up on the idea of nightlife, CityWalk still embraces it, and the variety of nightclubs has proven successful with both tourists and locals craving a safe and predictable entertainment environment. **CityWalk's Rising Star** (8 P.M.–2 A.M. daily, $7, 21 and over Fri.–Wed., 18 and over Thurs.) is the most recent addition, and it takes the karaoke bar concept to a new level; instead of singing along to plinky-plonky backing tracks, singers mount the stage to be accompanied by a live band. The **Red Coconut Club** (8 P.M.–2 A.M. Sun.–Thurs., 6 P.M.–2 A.M. Fri.–Sat., $7, 21 and over) was designed to capitalize on the ultra-lounge trend and emphasizes its fashionable atmosphere, VIP bottle service, and long martini list. DJs spin here, but dancing is best done at **The Groove** (9 P.M.–2 A.M. daily, $7, 21 and over), an enormous hit-driven dance club. Fans of live music should check out the lineup at **Hard Rock Live** (open only for concerts, ticket prices vary, all ages admitted); the huge modern venue hosts well-known touring bands and comedians and occasionally features local music as well.

Food

Nobody comes to a **Hard Rock Cafe** (11 A.M.–midnight or later daily, main courses from $12) for the food, but grabbing an expensive—and admittedly tasty—burger at this one is a must-do for rock-and-roll fans; this outpost of the international chain is the world's largest, and accordingly it has a most impressive collection of memorabilia.

There's something a little disturbing about tucking into "The Whaler" (a tilapia sandwich) or a "Natty Dread" (vegetable patties) while your little one noshes on "Jamacaroni and Cheese" and flocks of tourists take part in the beer and booze specials of "Red Stripe Rastafarian Thursday." At least it's disturbing to me. Still, as jarring as the theming of **Bob Marley – A Tribute to Freedom** (4:30 P.M.–2 A.M. daily, main courses from $9) may seem, the kitchen serves up some surprisingly tasty Jamaican dishes. I just wish they'd change the name to "A Taste of Babylon" or something like that.

Emeril's (lunch 11:30 A.M.–2 P.M. daily, dinner 5:30–10 P.M. daily, main courses from $18) is, of course, one of celebrity chef Emeril Lagasse's 10 restaurants, and the menu is predictably a combination of New Orleans flavors and contemporary cuisine. The stylish dining room can sometimes be deafeningly loud, but dishes like an andouille-crusted redfish are worth the hustle and bustle. Rumor has it that the billionth person to say "BAM!" on tasting their food gets a free dessert…at least it seems that way, judging by the tourists who think they're the first person ever to make that exclamation.

◀ **Latin Quarter** (5–10 P.M. daily, main courses from $15) is an oft-overlooked gem among CityWalk restaurants, probably because the pan-Latin menu goes well above and beyond the Tex-Mex fare one might expect here. Instead, Latin Quarter serves up a wide variety of excellent traditional dishes like churrasco skirt steak, paella, carne frita, and chorizo-topped snapper.

If you're headed to CityWalk for a night of entertainment but are interested in some different on-site dining options, the resort's three hotels have some impressive restaurants. **Emeril's Tchoup Chop** (Royal Pacific Resort, 5:30–10 P.M. Sun.–Thurs., 5:30–11 P.M. Fri.–Sat., main courses from $18) is a more upscale and quieter fine-dining experience than Lagasse's CityWalk boîte, with prices and dress code to match. The Orlando outpost of famed New York steakhouse **The Palm** (Hard Rock Hotel, 5–11 P.M. daily, main courses from $20) successfully captures the elegance and classic American menu of its namesake.

Shopping

Although it sort of feels like an outdoor mall, there's actually not all that much shopping to be done at CityWalk. However, if you want to get a tattoo—or just a tattoo-inspired T-shirt—**Hart & Huntington Tattoo Company** (11 A.M.–1 A.M. daily) has one of their three locations here; no, they don't film *Inked* here.

The Endangered Species Store (11 A.M.–11 P.M. daily) promotes a planet-in-peril theme by selling stuffed animals and eco-educational games and toys. There are also outlets for **Fossil** and clothing stores like **Fresh Produce** and **Tommy Bahama** as well as the Florida-based **Quiet Flight Surf Shop**.

ACCOMMODATIONS

Unlike Walt Disney World, Universal Orlando doesn't really mess around with "value" accommodations; whether due to limited real estate or the fact that dozens of moderate and inexpensive chain motels are located less than a half-mile from the park's entrance, the result is a trio of hotels that are unabashedly upscale. Guests staying at resort hotels can use their guest room keys as "Universal Express" passes, allowing them to bypass the line at the theme parks' major attractions. This perk, along with the availability of discounted ticket-accommodation packages, make an on-site stay an attractive option for some visitors, but again, there are considerably cheaper hotels nearby, most of which offer complimentary transportation to the park (and the Disney parks) as well as their own discount packages.

Resort Hotels

For on-site reservations, call 888/273-1311.

The best and most exciting of the three Universal Orlando resort hotels is the excellent ◖ **Hard Rock Hotel** (from $309 d), which incorporates the chain's rock-and-roll theming with extensive touches of modern luxury. Flat-panel TVs, in-room stereos, and deluxe contemporary furnishings make the spacious guest rooms welcoming and comfortable. The 12,000-square-foot pool at the Hard Rock is as glam as it gets; with water piped in underwater, high-tech and sumptuous cabanas, Jacuzzis, and a volleyball court, during the summer this pool is a destination in and of itself.

The **Loews Portofino Bay Resort** (from $339 d) is even pricier but is considerably more sedate and traditionally swanky. The recreation of a waterfront Italian village is something of a stretch (the designers even installed cobblestone sidewalks), but for a moment you almost believe that you're not a few hundred yards from roller coasters on one side and the Florida Turnpike on the other.

At the "low" end of the resort hotel offerings is **Loews Royal Pacific Resort** (from $274 d); ironically, it's also the most secluded and quiet. The Polynesian motif lends itself to long days lounging at the pool, sipping tropical drinks. The guest rooms, however, are decorated in neutral tones and dark woods, rather than tropical shades and lots of wicker.

Nearby Hotels

As mentioned earlier, there's no shortage of moderately priced chain hotels near Universal Orlando. There's also no abundance of remotely interesting places to stay. Most nearby hotels are located on the busy tourist strip of International Drive or the almost-as-overwhelmed Kirkman Road. Both the **Holiday Inn Hotel & Suites** (5905 Kirkman Rd., 407/351-3333, from $74 d) and the **Doubletree Hotel** (5780 Major Blvd., 407/351-1000, from $109 d) are located immediately adjacent to the park. The quality of the Holiday Inn isn't that high, but it's a decent budget option. The Doubletree gets high marks all around. A mile or so from the park entrance is the **Four Points by Sheraton Studio City** (5905 International Dr., 407/351-2100, from $125 d), which despite its Hollywood facade isn't all that glamorous, and the hotel can often be crowded with tour groups; nonetheless, guest rooms here are clean and reasonably appointed.

DINING NEAR THE RESORT

Orlando's "Restaurant Row"—home to a high concentration of upscale and midscale restaurants—is located in the tourist district along Sand Lake Road, near International Drive and the Orange County Convention Center.

INFORMATION AND SERVICES

As with the Disney parks, guide maps are easily available throughout any of the parks and can be found at restaurants, snack bars, and gift shops. The staff-to-guest ratio at Universal isn't quite as high as it is at Disney, and the crew here hasn't gone through the same sort of mission-critical training for customer service that Disney prides itself on, so your odds are a little higher that the person you randomly ask for help may neither know how to help you nor care to figure it out. Still, there are guest service stations at the entrances of both parks as well as in CityWalk.

Universal offers stroller, wheelchair, and locker rentals, and has a Family Services room at the entrance of each park with nursing facilities.

There's a day-boarding kennel facility located in the main parking garage; guests are required to provide food and occasionally come back during the day to walk their pets.

For more information, call the general information number at 407/363-8000 or visit the website at www.universalorlando.com.

GETTING THERE
By Air

There are two airports that serve the greater Orlando area, **Orlando International Airport** (MCO, One Airport Blvd., Orlando, 407/825-2001, www.orlandoairports.net) and **Orlando-Sanford International Airport** (SFB, 1200 Red Cleveland Blvd., Sanford, 407/585-4000, www.orlandosanfordairport.com). Universal Orlando and the nearby hotels on International Drive are only about 15 minutes from Orlando International Airport; the Sanford airport is 45 minutes away.

By Car

Universal Orlando Resort is located near the intersection of I-4 and International Drive.

GETTING AROUND

Due to its small size, Universal doesn't have any intraresort bus service, although there is a boat that ferries resort-hotel guests to and from the parks, and any visitor not staying at one of the resort's hotels will need to park in the massive parking structure at the resort's entrance and undertake the long walk to the park entrances. Parking is $12 and you'll park in a garage that allows access to Universal Studios Orlando, Islands of Adventure, and CityWalk. I'd recommend, however, springing for valet parking ($20), which brings you into the resort right at the entrance to CityWalk. The reduced walk may not seem like that big of a deal when you're first coming into the park, but the $8 difference will seem well worth it after a day on your feet.

SeaWorld Orlando

For almost a decade—from its opening in 1973 to the launch of Epcot Center in 1982—SeaWorld Orlando was comfortably "the other Orlando theme park." It was the place to take the kids on a long weekend after the treasures of the Magic Kingdom had been exhausted, or the place you went if you couldn't quite afford the ticket prices at Disney. Even after Disney's other parks opened and Universal Orlando got off the ground, SeaWorld just went along its merry way, putting on Shamu shows and letting you ride an escalator through a shark tank. In 1998, though, it appeared that someone at the park realized SeaWorld was in danger of becoming an antiquated oddity, classed alongside old-school attractions like Gatorland, and so Journey to Atlantis—SeaWorld's first thrill ride—was opened. After that first water coaster came the high-speed Kraken steel coaster as well as a renewed focus on conservation messages in their animal exhibits. SeaWorld had renewed itself in terms of vitality and relevance, and the expansion continued to include the dolphin-interaction experiences at Discovery Cove and the water-park fun at Aquatica.

While the resort is still definitely the lesser of the "big three," it certainly warrants consideration on any visitor's itinerary. The sea-mammal shows at the main park are truly unique, especially when combined with roller coaster thrills, and Discovery Cove is an absolute must-visit experience. The various pricing schemes SeaWorld offers also make it an incredible bargain.

Standard admission to SeaWorld is $75 adults and $65 children, but online discounts are available, and the ticket is good for two days of admission rather than just one. Multipark ticket packages can be constructed that add on admission to Busch Gardens or Aquatica ($100 adults, $90 children) as well as Busch Gardens and Aquatica ($135 adults, $125 children). Packages with Discovery Cove admission are also available, beginning at $259. Florida residents can get additional discounts, and annual passes are also quite a bargain.

SeaWorld also sells "Orlando FlexTicket" packages, which provide unlimited admission for two weeks to SeaWorld, Aquatica, both Universal parks, and Wet 'n' Wild for $235 adults and $215 children. For an additional $45, you can add Busch Gardens Tampa to the list, and they'll provide round-trip shuttle transportation at no extra cost.

SeaWorld has no on-site accommodations, and as for nearby dining, you'll be heading for the International Drive area.

SEAWORLD ADVENTURE PARK

This is the park people are referring to when they're talking about SeaWorld. There's an impressive slate of trained animal shows featuring dolphins, sea lions, and of course Shamu as well as informative and educational sea-life exhibits and a steadily growing roster of thrill rides—the newest coaster, Manta, opened in 2009. While the park isn't quite as idyllic as one might hope from a nature-oriented attraction, it's lushly landscaped, and the animals all seem to be treated respectfully with clean modern habitats.

Rides

Although most thrill-seekers head straight for the high-speed steel coaster known as **Kraken**, I have to give the nod to **Journey to Atlantis** when it comes to picking SeaWorld's best ride. Sure, dropping 145 feet at 65 mph makes for a winning ride by nearly any yardstick, but there's something about Atlantis' combination of the dark ride theme, the log flume soaking, and roller coaster speed—not to mention the enormous fake-out at the end—that makes the ride a truly unique experience.

A somewhat more sedate experience can be had at **Wild Arctic,** which combines a motion-simulator ride with a walk-through animal exhibit filled with polar bears, walruses, and beluga whales.

A 140-foot-high flying steel coaster called **Manta** that out-adrenalines Kraken opened in 2009.

Shows

The heart of SeaWorld is its variety of animal shows. Although all are centrally focused on the amazing abilities of the animals—and the unique capabilities of the trainers and water acrobats that join them in the shows—each has a somewhat different premise and emphasis. **Believe** and the seasonal **Shamu Rocks** are both held in the spacious **Shamu Stadium.** The enormous facility—and its seven-million-gallon tank—is needed to accommodate the iconic killer whales who star in the shows. Of the two, Shamu Rocks is definitely the cornier, themed around a rock concert motif with a fantastic light show and less-than-fantastic tunes. Believe is all about Shamu, casting aside story and theme in favor of dazzling trainer-animal choreography and visual effects. **Blue Horizons** is a fast-paced show designed around some stunning dolphin tricks; the song-driven plot has something to do with a young girl's vivid dreams and is incredibly hard to follow, but the dazzling costumes and gymnastic interplay of the dolphins and the human actors make the story more than secondary.

Animal Exhibits

Also integral to SeaWorld's identity are the

various animal exhibits, which allow visitors to get up close to various denizens of the deep. All are pretty self-explanatory—you can see manatees at **Manatee Rescue,** penguins at the **Penguin Encounter,** and stingrays in the **Stingray Lagoon.** The chance to touch and feed the dolphins at **Dolphin Cove** and the thrill of traveling through an underwater tube while sharks swim overhead in the superlative **Shark Encounter** attraction make both of these exhibits must-sees.

Food

The menu of pasta, steak, chicken, and ironically, seafood at ◖ **Sharks Underwater Grill** (lunch and dinner, main courses from $14) is decent enough, but its the dining room—in which one wall is shared with the glass of an enormous shark-filled aquarium—that's the real attraction here. If being surrounded by marine life all day has dampened your appetite for seafood, **Voyager's** (lunch and dinner, main courses from $9) has a limited selection of home-style barbecue dishes served with watermelon and grilled corn-on-the-cob, as well as salads.

SeaWorld also has a few special dining events on a daily basis; the **Bud 'n' BBQ All-You-Care-to-Eat Family Picnic** (11:30 A.M.–4 P.M. daily, $15.95 adults, $8.95 children 3–9, reservations necessary) is the best value, with the smoked and grilled selections from Voyager's augmented by burgers and hot dogs. Soft drinks are included in the price, but beer is not. The **Makahiki Luau** (nightly at sunset, Seafire Inn, $46 adults, $29 children 3–9) is as campy as the name implies, with nearly every cliché of the South Pacific—hula dances, giant tiki torches, and more—trotted out to accompany your feasting on barbecue spareribs, fried rice, mahimahi, and "Hawaiian chicken." Obviously, you won't actually be in the tank when you **Dine With Shamu** (at the killer whale habitat, $42 adults, $22 children 3–9), but the poolside tables at this buffet-style dining experience provide an up-close look at SeaWorld's star; the behind-the-scenes look makes up for the pedestrian selection of pasta, chicken, and turkey dishes.

Special Events

Bud 'n' BBQ (Feb.) celebrates the all-American trifecta of beer, smoked meat, and country music, while **Viva La Musica** (Apr.) is a Latin music event that usually brings in at least a couple of high-profile pop stars for performances.

During the summer, SeaWorld stays open late for **SeaWorld After Dark** (late May–early Sept.), which allows guests to ride rides, do a little extra shopping, and see seasonal shows like Shamu Rocks. On weekends in October, kids can don costumes and trick-or-treat throughout the park as part of **SeaWorld's Halloween Spooktacular.**

The Polar Express Experience (Dec.) transforms the Wild Arctic attraction into a recreation of the beloved children's story.

AQUATICA

As far as water parks go, SeaWorld's Aquatica (5800 Water Play Way, hours vary seasonally, open year-round except a few dates in winter, $44.95 adults, $38.95 children) is a far more attractive proposition than the crowded mayhem of International Drive's Wet 'n' Wild, and the added element of live animals—from Commerson's dolphins and tropical fish to a wide variety of exotic birds—even sets it apart from the two Disney water parks. But still, a water park's a water park, and Aquatica's main attraction is the number of opportunities it provides visitors to get wet.

Rides and Slides

By far the most unique slide at Aquatica is the **Dolphin Plunge,** which races you down one of two side-by-side tube slides—right through a water habitat filled with dolphins. Although you'll likely be going too fast to really observe them at play, the underwater sensation is completely unique.

More traditional attractions at Aquatica include the side-by-side wave pools and sunbathing area of **Cutback Cove & Big Surf Shores,** the splashing river rafting adventure of **Roa's Rapids,** and **Whanau Way,** an enormous, four-slide tower.

a dolphin performing at SeaWorld

There's also the **Loggerhead Lane** lazy river and two kid-friendly areas.

Food

Dining options are fairly limited at Aquatica; the **WaterStone Grill** serves sandwiches and salads, and the **Mango Market** has pizzas, wraps, and chicken tenders. Guests committed to an entire day's visit tend to opt for the **Banana Beach Cookout,** which sells full-day passes, allowing unlimited noshing on their barbecue, burgers, and dogs for $19.95 (adults) and $9.95 (kids).

◖ DISCOVERY COVE

There are no sky-high roller coasters or cartoon characters at SeaWorld's Discovery Cove, but that's sort of the point. More a secluded natural oasis than a typical theme park, the marquee attraction here is the opportunity for one-on-one animal encounters, including a 30-minute swim session with dolphins, snorkeling among hundreds of brightly colored tropical fish, and wading in a lagoon filled with rays. In addition to the up-close animal interactions, the lush grounds also house an aviary and a beautiful temperature-controlled swimming area.

The point of a visit to Discovery Cove is to experience a day of exclusive relaxation, much as one might find when visiting a private island. As such, admission prices are all-inclusive; it's $289 for a day that incorporates the dolphin encounter and $189 without it, although I can't imagine coming and not participating in this one-of-a-kind experience. Food and drinks throughout the day, gear rental for snorkeling, towels, lockers, beach chairs, and even sunscreen are included in the price of admission. (Private cabanas are available for an additional rental charge.) Even better, admission to Discovery Cove also includes 14 days of consecutive admission to SeaWorld Orlando or Busch Gardens in Tampa. Reservations are required and should be made well in advance, as the park is filled to capacity most days; reservations made more than 100 days in advance are eligible for discounted rates. There are also occasional seasonal discounts.

The **Trainer for a Day** program adds an

additional semiprivate dolphin interaction (you can ride them!), a behind-the-scenes tour and Q&A session with a trainer, and a gift bag; adding this program brings the total admission fee to $488.

INFORMATION AND SERVICES

There are guest service kiosks at the entrance of both SeaWorld and Aquatica, and park maps are readily available throughout both parks. Guests enjoying the day at Discovery Cove will find that from the moment they check in at the reservation desk, they will have attentive service throughout the day. For inquiries in advance of your visit, www.seaworld.com is a good source for FAQs and other information, and the park has a guest service line at 888/800-5447.

SeaWorld offers stroller, wheelchair, and locker rental as well as kennel service, located just outside the main entrance.

GETTING THERE AND AROUND
By Air

There are two airports that serve the greater Orlando area, **Orlando International Airport** (MCO, One Airport Blvd., Orlando, 407/825-2001, www.orlandoairports.net) and **Orlando-Sanford International Airport** (SFB, 1200 Red Cleveland Blvd., Sanford, 407/585-4000, www.orlandosanfordairport.com). SeaWorld and the nearby hotels on International Drive are only about 15 minutes from Orlando International Airport; the Sanford airport is 45 minutes away.

By Car

SeaWorld is located just off International Drive near the intersection of I-4 and State Road 528 (the Beach Line Expressway toll road). Parking is $12, and your parking pass can be used at both Aquatica and SeaWorld. Parking at Discovery Cove is free.

International Drive Area

Somewhere there's an urban dictionary where the phrase "tourist trap" is accompanied by a photo of the garish gash of transient commerce known as I-Drive. Jammed side-by-side along the several miles of this strip is a seemingly endless agglomeration of buffet restaurants, T-shirt shops, tchotchke dealers, mini-golf courses, cheap hotels, sports bars, and bargain steakhouses. It's nearly unavoidable for visitors who venture out of the Disney cocoon for visits to Universal or SeaWorld.

ATTRACTIONS
Wet 'n' Wild

Owned by Universal Orlando—and therefore eligible for various add-on ticket discounts—Wet 'n' Wild (6200 International Dr., 407/351-1800, hours vary seasonally, park open year-round, $44.95 adults, $38.95 children, kids 2 and under free) is an I-Drive institution; it was opened in 1977 by SeaWorld creator George Millay and is generally thought to be the first large-scale water park in the United States. Accordingly, Wet 'n' Wild's original incarnation set the tone for its many followers, and its expansion over the years has found it filling every nook and cranny of its 60-acre property with a dizzying array of water rides. There are more than 20 different attractions at Wet 'n' Wild, and nearly every one of them involves some variation on hurtling down a wet slide at top speed. There are some exceptions, though, in the handful of skiing activities that take place in and around the property's lake as well as the 17,000-square-foot wave pool. Despite its iconic status among water parks, it must be said that the park's amazing rates for weekday annual passes—available for an additional $5—mean that during the summer, large groups of teenagers descend on Wet 'n' Wild en masse, making a day at the park a little less family-friendly than some folks might care for.

INTERNATIONAL DRIVE AREA   **53**

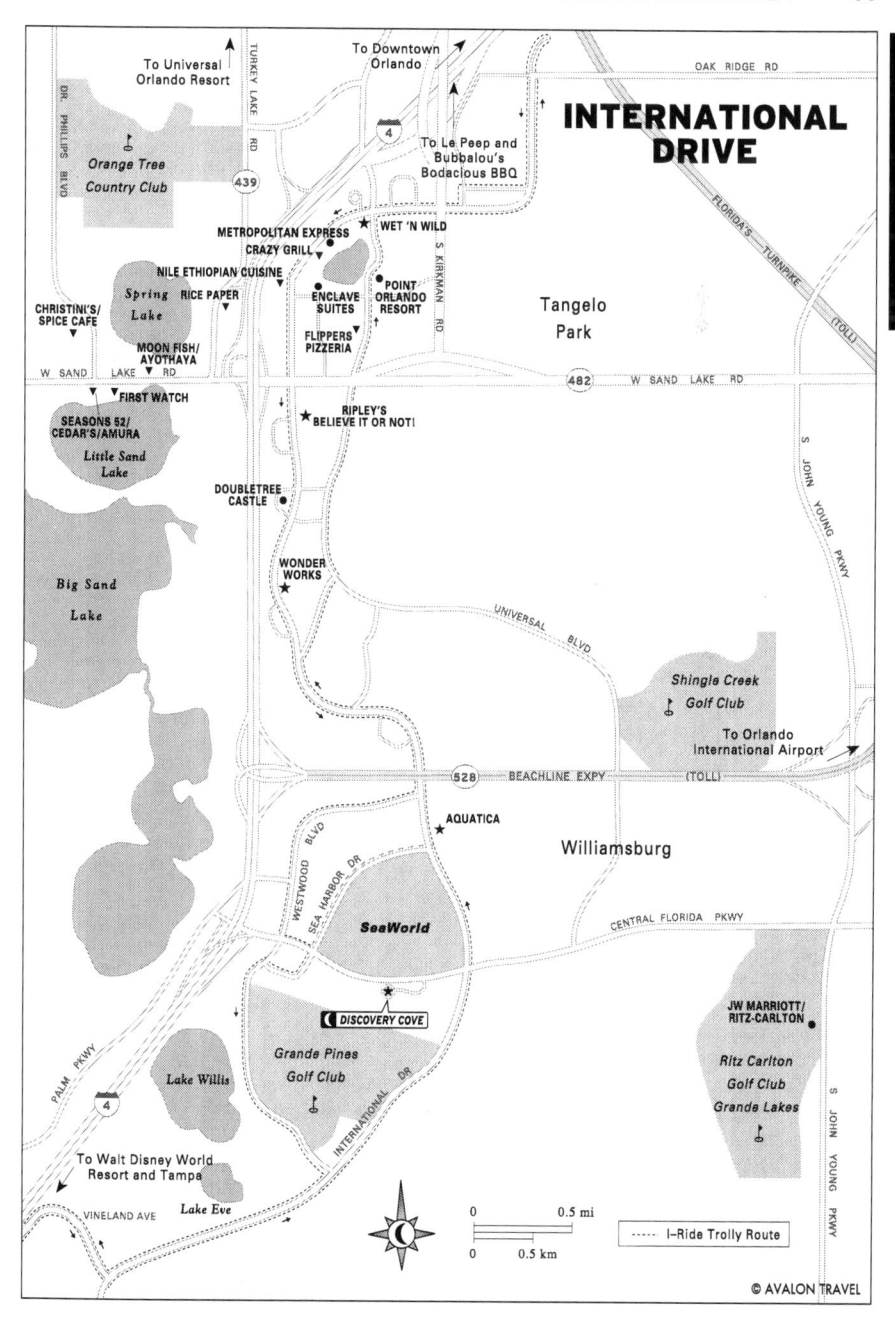

OTHER NEARBY ATTRACTIONS

If eight theme parks, four water parks, and all their attendant distractions aren't enough to occupy your Central Florida vacation, there are a couple of other area attractions to check out.

GATORLAND

Founded in 1949, Gatorland (14501 S. Orange Blossom Tr., Kissimmee, 407/855-5496, 9 A.M.-5 P.M. daily, $22.99 adults, $14.99 children) is a Central Florida icon, attracting Northern tourists who made their way down the once-scenic Orange Blossom Trail decades before the Magic Kingdom was even a glint in Walt Disney's eye. The basic premise is unchanged: Visitors tromp around decks that overlook lakes filled with gators, occasionally taking time out to watch one of the many feeding shows that happen throughout the day. There are also gator-wrestling exhibitions and an extensive trail-and-boardwalk system that winds through the 110-acre property.

ZIPLINE SAFARI

Zipline Safari (4755 N. Kenansville Rd., St. Cloud, 866/854-3837, www.floridaecosafaris.com, groups depart hourly 10 A.M.-4 P.M., $85, participants must be at least 10 years old and weigh 70-275 pounds) is one of the most recent additions to the to-do list of active travelers in the area. It's the only zipline in Florida... and the only one in the world designed for flat land. The lines run through the forests and ranchlands of Osceola County, hurtling riders at speeds of up to 20 mph as they hang more than 50 feet in the air.

Wonder Works

The garish upside-down building on the side of I-Drive? That's Wonder Works (9067 International Dr., 407/351-8800, 9 A.M.–midnight daily, adults $19.95, children $14.95), an attraction that takes all the interactive exhibits frequently found in science centers and children's museums and strips all the educational value from them. The facility itself has seen better days, and the entertainment value hardly holds up for repeat visits, although as a rainy-day time-killer it's not too terrible. Games of laser tag can be appended to the admission fee for an additional $4.95.

Ripley's Believe It Or Not!

It wouldn't be a tourist trap without a Ripley's Believe It Or Not! (8201 International Blvd., 407/351-5803, 9:30 A.M.–midnight daily, $18.95 adults, $11.95 children, kids 3 and under free), now, would it? This "Odditorium" is much like other Ripley's outposts in other tourist-swarmed locales, featuring shrunken heads, a three-legged man, a Rolls Royce made out of matchsticks, a portrait of the Mona Lisa made out of burned toast, and other sublimely ridiculous things. The building is hard to miss, as it appears to be sinking into the ground.

ACCOMMODATIONS

The hokey architecture of the **Doubletree Castle** (8629 International Dr., 407/345-1511, from $150 d) fits right in with the overblown atmosphere of International Drive. Although a stay here probably won't make anyone feel like royalty, the Renaissance-era styling and mass-market luxury touches make it one of the better values on the tourist strip.

Enclave Suites (6165 Carrier Dr., 407/351-1155, from $79 d) is a pretty basic hotel, with decent—if slightly worn—guest rooms. About half of the guest rooms are regular hotel accommodations, the rest are kitchen-equipped suites in studio, one-bedroom, and two-bedroom sizes. There are four pools on the property, as well as a tennis court, game room, and playground.

For true budget travelers, the motel-style **Metropolitan Express** (6323 International Dr., 407/351-4430, from $60 d) is a good option. Although the guest rooms aren't going to win any awards for spaciousness or style, they've got all the basics, and the hotel has a free continental breakfast buffet and complimentary shuttles to the Disney parks.

The ◖ **Point Orlando Resort** (7385 Universal Blvd., 407/956-2000, studio suites from $109) is surprisingly quiet considering its location in the thick of the I-Drive action. The relatively new, all-suite property has studio, one-, and two-bedroom "condotel" accommodations, all of which have full kitchens, flat-screen televisions and laundry facilities. Guest rooms and public areas are clean and contemporary.

Those looking to escape the masses of budget travelers should head for the **JW Marriott** (407/206-2300, from $219 d) or the **Ritz-Carlton** (407/206-2400, from $239 d), both of which are located a few miles away at **Grande Lakes Orlando** (4040 Central Florida Pkwy., www.grandelakes.com), a 500-acre golf and convention resort set on a nature preserve. The combined amenities of the two five-star hotels include eleven restaurants, a spa, meeting facilities, a fly-fishing school, a Greg Norman–designed golf course, three tennis courts, bocce ball, carriage rides, three pools…yeah, you won't need to leave the property. It goes without saying that the guest rooms and suites are up to the high standards set by each of the top-shelf chains.

FOOD

It's somewhat ironic that a number of excellent restaurants have popped up in the shadow of three people-pleasing theme parks, but that's just what's happened along Orlando's own **Restaurant Row,** a strip of Sand Lake Road west of I-4. There are a couple of dozen praiseworthy spots in this small area (which also happens to be close to the upscale neighborhoods of Dr. Phillips and Bay Hill), and by all means, if you're wondering where to eat, aim your car here rather than the garish tourist strip of International Drive. Although there are a handful of neat spots on I-Drive, some of the best restaurants in Orlando are located along Sand Lake Road.

Breakfast

Two national chains have outlets near the I-Drive area that provide an excellent alternative to the IHOPs, Denny's, and doughnut shops that are prevalent in the area. **First Watch** (7500 W. Sand Lake Rd., 407/363-5622, 7 A.M.–2:30 P.M. daily, main courses from $7) is a Florida-based chain that emphasizes fresh ingredients, a wide selection of healthy breakfast options, and unique preparations like "chickichanga," with scrambled eggs, chorizo, chilis, cheese, and avocado piled into a tortilla. Standard breakfast fare is also available in ample portions. **Le Peep** (4666 S. Kirkman Rd., 407/291-4580, 6:30 A.M.–2:30 P.M. Mon.–Fri., 7 A.M.–2:30 P.M. Sat.–Sun., main courses from $6) adds crepes and a variety of pancakes to the typical breakfast menu, but the main reason to head here is for the excellent coffee and decadent Gooey Buns, which are English muffins broiled and topped with brown sugar, cinnamon, cream cheese, and skillet-fried apples.

The locally-owned **Florida Waffle Shop** (4192 Conroy Rd., 407/226-1400, 7 A.M.–2:30 P.M. daily, main courses from $6) specializes in waffles, and tops the Belgian beasts with any combination of fruit, nuts, and whipped cream you can come up with. Omelets, pancakes, and eggs-and-bacon plates are also available.

American

Bubbalou's Bodacious BBQ (5818 Conroy Rd., 407/295-1212, 10 A.M.–9:30 P.M. Mon.–Thurs., 10 A.M.–10:30 P.M. Fri.–Sat., 11 A.M.–9 P.M. Sun., main courses from $5) is a locally-based chain that serves decent smoked-meat meals along with things like sausage sandwiches and fried catfish, which is all well and good. However, the main reason to darken the door of this restaurant is its fried corn on the cob; the buttery, crispy treat is as near a perfect accompaniment to a pile of brisket as yet created.

Orlando is home to Darden International, the parent company of casual dining behemoths like Olive Garden and Red Lobster. So the opening of a new Darden concept restaurant in the area wasn't much of a surprise. Both the concept and the quality of

◖ **Seasons 52** (7700 W. Sand Lake Rd., 407/354-5212, 11:30 A.M.–2:30 P.M. and 5–10 P.M. Mon.–Fri., 11:30 A.M.–11 P.M. Sat., 11:30 A.M.–10 P.M. Sun., main courses from $16) were unexpected of the company behind the "never-ending pasta bowl." Every item on the Seasons 52 menu clocks in at 475 calories or less, but it's far from an ascetic dining experience. The emphasis is on seasonal dishes, hence the "Seasons" of the name, and a menu that's tweaked for freshness on a weekly basis, hence the "52." The result is an exquisite and upscale dining experience that's actually about the food rather than about indulgence. Although the menu regularly changes, there's always an abundance of fish and seafood dishes as well as tasty and filling entrée-sized salads. Even steak and poultry manage to squeeze their way onto the calorie-restricted menu, and the rich and perfectly portioned desserts are served in shot glass-sized containers.

Steak and Seafood

Although there are a handful of other Brazilian-style churrascarias along I-Drive, none can match the friendliness and value at ◖ **Crazy Grill** (7048 International Dr., 407/354-4404, 5:30–10 P.M. Tues.–Fri., 1–10 P.M. Sat.–Sun., $26.95 per person). In keeping with the style, each diner is given a plate and a cork; the cork is green on one side, red on the other. Turn the cork so the green side is up and a cavalcade of grilled meats will begin to pile up on your plate, fresh from the kitchen. A dozen different cuts of slow-roasted meat will be offered continually, from flank steak and chicken to some mouth-watering sausage. Turn the cork to red when you need a break. Delicious bread is served tableside, and there's a salad bar filled with fresh vegetables if you feel your heart beginning to rebel. Although it's considerably cheaper than some of the other churrascarias in the area, the food is still exceptional, and the laid-back atmosphere and affable service make for a casual dining experience.

In the I-Drive/Restaurant Row area, there's a Bonefish Grill, a FishBones, and then there's **Moon Fish** (7525 W. Sand Lake Rd., 407/363-7262, 5–10 P.M. Sun.–Thurs., 5–11 P.M. Fri.–Sat., main courses from $22); if you're craving high-end preparations of seafood, the latter should be your destination. Asian touches abound on the menu, but there's also a solid selection of steaks and chops. The raw bar serves up phenomenal oysters.

Italian

If the baroque decor of the sumptuous dining room at **Christini's** (7600 Dr. Philips Blvd., 407/345-8770, 6 P.M.–midnight daily, main courses from $30) doesn't clue you in that you're in for some old-school fine dining, then perhaps the strolling musicians or the gift of a red rose to lady diners should do the trick. Owner Chris Christini prides himself on the "classical" atmosphere of his restaurant; unfortunately, his kitchen is seldom bothered to learn new tricks. Heavily sauced "gourmet" pasta and meat dishes barely surpass the quality delivered in family-style chains like Buca di Beppo. Charm and ambiance can take you a long way, but at the prices charged at Christini's, one would expect far better food.

For something a little more relaxed, the best pizza in the area is **Flippers Pizzeria** (7480 Universal Blvd., 407/351-5643, 11 A.M.–midnight or later daily). With six theme-park area locations, you'll undoubtedly be able to get one of their fantastic pies to your hotel room door.

Asian

Ayothaya (7555 W. Sand Lake Rd., 407/345-0040, 11 A.M.–3 P.M. and 5–10 P.M. Mon.–Fri., noon–10 P.M. Sat.–Sun., main courses from $10) serves excellent Thai food in teak-heavy surroundings; in addition to the standard curries, soups, and noodle dishes, they also offer a number of specialties like spicy duck and steamed fish.

◖ **Amura** (7786 W. Sand Lake Rd., 407/370-0007, lunch 11:30 A.M.–2:30 P.M. Mon.–Fri., noon–3 P.M. Sat.–Sun., dinner 5–10 P.M. daily, sushi rolls from $9) is consistently touted as one of the best sushi restaurants in Orlando, which is an opinion that's difficult to argue with. From the modern decor and the see-and-be-seen atmosphere, the vibe is decidedly hip and upscale—they even refer to their sushi preparations as "high-definition"…whatever that means. The staff is exceedingly friendly and will even guide novices through the menu's wide range of options. Masterfully constructed rolls are brimming with flavor, and some of the more exclusive preparations, like the Coco-Mango roll (tuna, salmon, mango, coconut, and cilantro), are absolutely mind-blowing.

Those craving Vietnamese cuisine in Orlando usually head toward downtown's Little Vietnam neighborhood; however, the recent addition of **Rice Paper** (7637 Turkey Lake Rd., 407/352-4700, 11 A.M.–9 P.M. Mon.–Thurs., 11 A.M.–10 P.M. Fri.–Sat., noon–9 P.M. Sun., main courses from $12) to the Restaurant Row area has given theme-park visitors a much closer option. An extensive menu of pho, curries, clay pots, and other Vietnamese staples is prepared expertly, although service here can sometimes be a little scattered.

Other International

Cedar's (7732 W. Sand Lake Rd., 407/351-6000, 11:30 A.M.–10:30 P.M. Mon.–Fri., noon–2 A.M. Sat., noon–9 P.M. Sun., main courses from $16) presents a selection of authentic Middle Eastern and Mediterranean dishes in a stylish atmosphere. Saturday nights feature live belly dancing performances.

The cafeteria-style **Spice Cafe** (7536 Dr. Phillips Dr., 407/264-0205, 11 A.M.–10 P.M. Tues.–Sat., noon–10 P.M. Sun., main courses from $8) may not win any points for atmosphere, but this quick-service Indian restaurant has the best malai kofta in Orlando, and is one of the only places in town that has bhel puri on the menu. Tandoor-cooked meats and breads are also available—the tandoor is in plain sight, allowing the mysteries of naan-making to be revealed—as well as a standard selection of north Indian dishes.

Finding an Ethiopian restaurant tucked away among the ticky-tacky businesses of International Drive is something of a surprise, but right there, sitting next door to an Irish pub, is the family-run **Nile Ethiopian Cuisine** (7040 International Dr., 407/354-0026, 5–10 P.M. Mon.–Fri., 11 A.M.–midnight Sat.–Sun., main courses from $12). Food is served family-style and utensil-free, leaving you to sop up the richly spiced and delicious marinated meats and vegetables with the spongy sour injera bread. Although many of the dishes are based around poultry and beef, there are a number of vegetarian selections available as well. For a treat, finish off the meal with traditional Ethiopian coffee service.

METRO ORLANDO AND CENTRAL FLORIDA

Theme parks are a big part of Orlando's reputation among travelers, but not everyone who comes to the "City Beautiful" is interested in roller coasters and character breakfasts.

Despite, or perhaps because of, the proximity of the resorts and theme parks, the city of Orlando has a distinct flavor that combines the urban flair of a growing midsize city and the ticky-tacky anonymity of sprawling indistinct suburbs. The downtown area is compact, serving as a business hub during the day and a drinking destination at night; although considerable efforts have been made to give the city's core a high-density residential feel, it nonetheless feels as if it's constantly hosting guests. Immediately outside the core, however, is where the city shines, with diverse neighborhoods housing everything from a bustling Vietnamese American district to art galleries, craft-beer bars, and a wide range of dining options.

Although functionally suburbs of Orlando, the scenic towns of Winter Park and Maitland have distinct identities from the "big" city, combining tree-lined streets, high-end shopping, historic buildings, and stunning museums.

Just beyond metropolitan Orlando is a wide array of outdoor activities, and several of the state's most accessible and beautiful natural springs are within a 45-minute drive of downtown. Also nearby are quaint towns like DeLand and Mount Dora, which give the visitor insight into Old Florida charm. And for something completely different, a stroll through the spiritualist community of Cassadaga could result in you leaving Florida

© JASON FERGUSON

HIGHLIGHTS

◖ **Loch Haven Park:** Near downtown Orlando, this park is home to several art museums, theaters, and the Orlando Science Center. While it may be lacking in some of the typical accoutrements of a city park – for instance, there are no slides or merry-go-rounds – the wide-open spaces are great for picnicking, and the numerous cultural opportunities here make it well worth exploring (page 64).

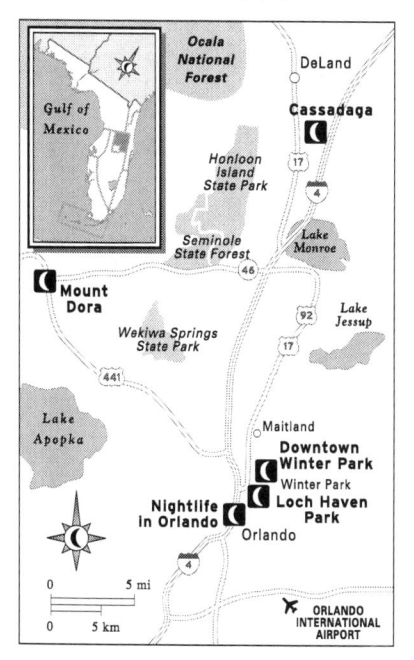

◖ **Downtown Winter Park:** Located just past the Orlando city limits, Winter Park got its start as a resort town preferred by upper-crust New Englanders in the early 1900s, and to this day, the scenic suburb is considered the toniest and nicest of all of Orlando's neighborhoods. The tree-lined downtown area is great for window-shopping and sightseeing (page 65).

◖ **Nightlife in Orlando:** Unlike any other city in Florida, Orlando's downtown district transforms every weekend night and many weekday nights into a compact and vibrant nightlife district, with dozens of bars, nightclubs, and restaurants competing for the attention and business of the throngs of young people who flock here to drink, dance, see concerts, and cut loose (page 69).

◖ **Cassadaga:** Few areas can claim to be home to a community of spiritualists and psychics, and the presence of one just a few miles from the gates of Walt Disney World is evidence to counter people's preconceptions about Orlando and Central Florida (page 83).

◖ **Mount Dora:** With a downtown district that's right out of a historic small-town postcard, the charming lakeside city of Mount Dora seems as if it was transported from some halcyon vision of Old Florida. Appropriately enough, one of the main attractions here is shopping the numerous antique stores and craft shops (page 84).

LOOK FOR ◖ TO FIND RECOMMENDED SIGHTS, ACTIVITIES, DINING, AND LODGING.

---

with a balanced aura to complement your sunburned skin.

HISTORY

Even given the relatively slim histories of Florida towns, Orlando is a notably young city. A rural farm town through most of the 19th century, the city didn't really begin to take shape until after the Civil War, when citrus farming began in earnest in the area. Two legendary freezes in the winter of 1894 took out most of the area's independent citrus growers, but ironically that disaster actually accelerated Orlando's growth as a citrus-producing region. Wealthy landowners like Dr. Philip Phillips not only took over the abandoned groves but implemented a number of industrial innovations in the packing and canning areas that allowed citrus from throughout Central Florida to be processed in Orlando.

60 WALT DISNEY WORLD & ORLANDO

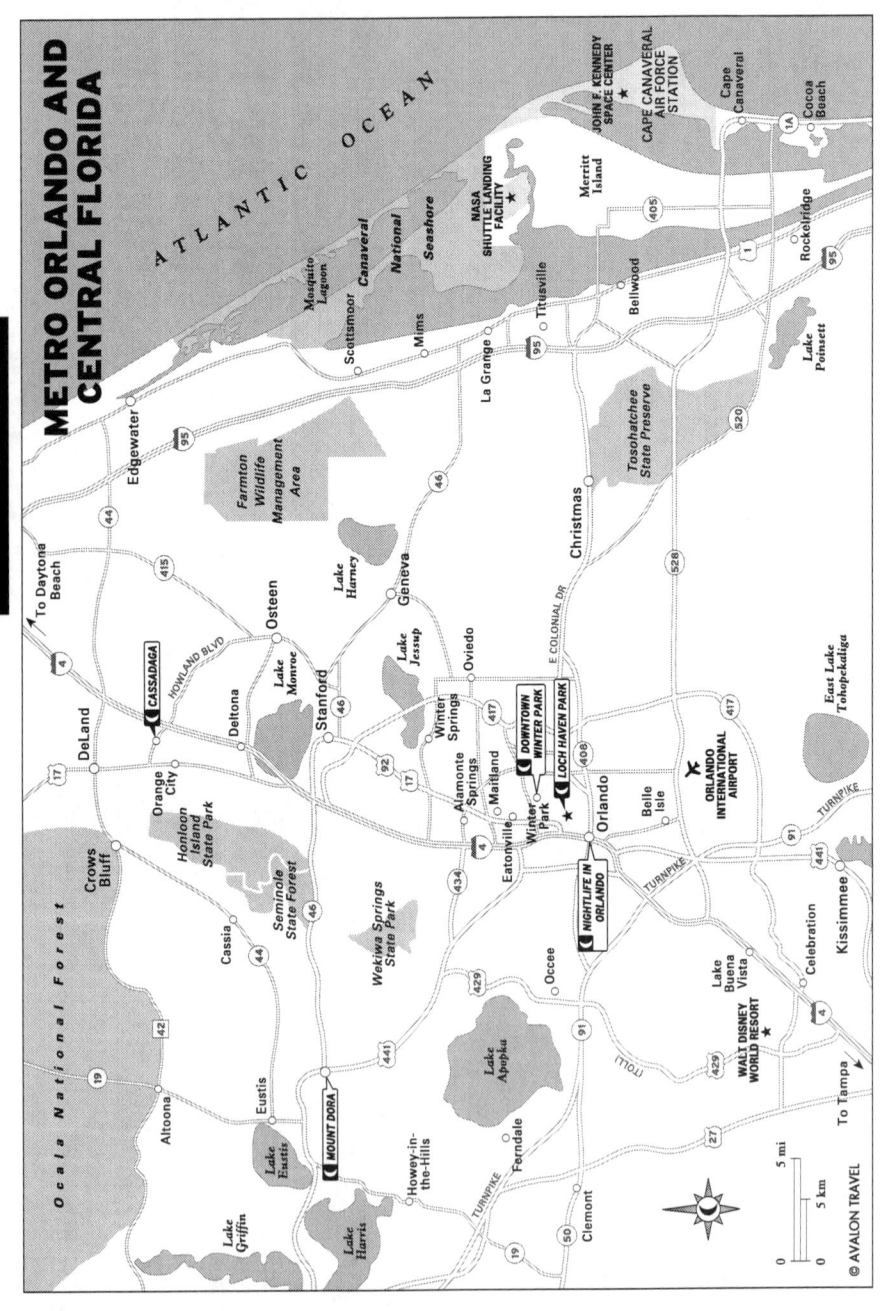

METRO ORLANDO

METRO ORLANDO AND CENTRAL FLORIDA

The growth of the citrus industry coincided with the first great Florida Land Boom in the early 20th century, and during that period, the city's municipal facilities grew considerably with the addition of a large public library, a performing arts hall, and more. In the 1950s, aerospace company Martin Marietta opened a plant in the Orlando area, complementing the air defense operations then based at McCoy Air Force Base (currently the site of Orlando International Airport), laying the groundwork for the region's role in the technology and defense sectors, a role most profoundly exhibited by the presence on the coast of Cape Canaveral and NASA.

Of course, when the Walt Disney Company started buying up land south of Orlando in the mid-1960s for what would become Walt Disney World, Orlando was set on an entirely different path. Although the aerospace and engineering industry has quite a presence in the area, millions of tourists don't flock to the city every year to watch missiles get designed. Nonetheless, the Orlando that could have been is still very much a part of the city's current makeup, and even if Disney had decided to build a park in Tampa or Tallahassee, the "City Beautiful" would likely still be one of Florida's largest and most vibrant towns.

PLANNING YOUR TIME

A few days in the Orlando and Central Florida area is all one needs to get a taste for this part of the state. Make a home base in central Orlando, and devote a day to seeing the sights there; another day can be devoted to exploring Winter Park and Maitland, and a third day could be spent in Cassadaga and nearby DeLand or trolling the antique malls of Mount Dora.

ORIENTATION

Downtown Orlando is approximately 22 miles (20 minutes' drive) northeast of the Walt Disney World Resort. The core downtown area is compact and bisected by north-south Orange Avenue and east-west Central Avenue. This core is actually a few blocks south of the main east-west thoroughfare, Colonial Drive, which intersects with north-south Mills Avenue (also known as U.S. 17/92) and I-4. U.S. 17/92 will take you north into Winter Park and Maitland, which are about 5 miles (10 minutes) from downtown, while I-4 continues northeast toward DeLand. Mount Dora is approximately 30 miles to the west-northwest of central Orlando.

Sights

ORLANDO

Before there was Walt Disney World, there was a growing city named Orlando, a city that was beginning to make a name for itself as a center for aeronautical and military technology. Had the Mouse not planted its oversized shoes a few miles south of Orlando, it's likely the city would have continued on its steady path of growth and would today be a respectable midsize burg in the heart of Central Florida. However, that's not what happened, and today, Orlando is immediately associated with theme parks and family fun with little thought given to the impressive slate of sights, attractions, and cultural activities that have nothing whatsoever to do with roller coasters or animated creatures. While the city's leaders have long been content to let tourism run the economic engine here, residents and adventurous travelers have learned that even without those theme parks to the south, the city is well-deserving of vacationers' attention.

Downtown Orlando

Most visitors to downtown Orlando are there for one of two reasons. Either they're conducting business, or they've sought respite from the theme parks, thinking that the city center might contain something of interest. While the former may well find success in their

62 WALT DISNEY WORLD & ORLANDO

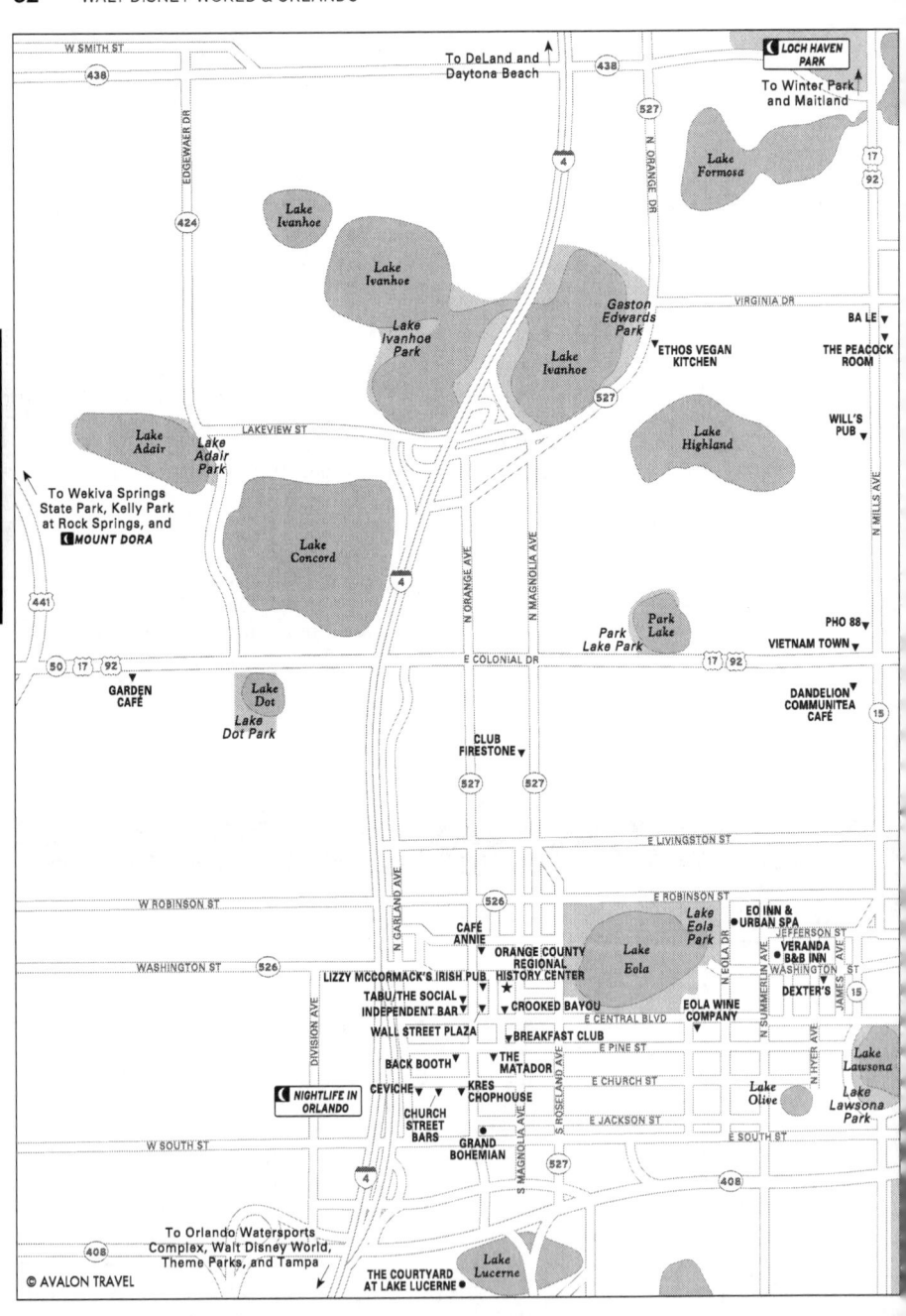

SIGHTS   **63**

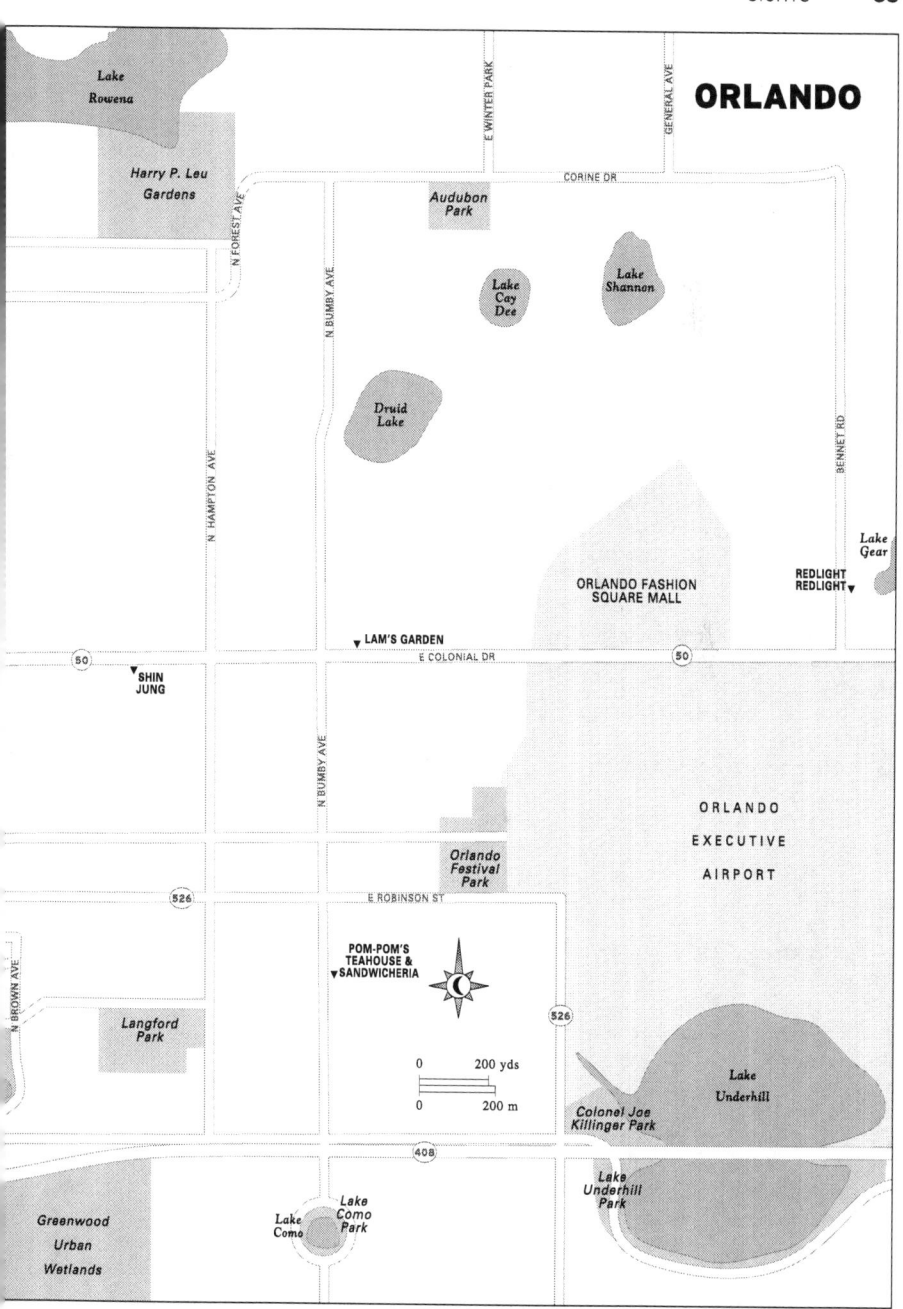

ORLANDO

deal-making, those in the latter group are likely to be sorely disappointed. Still, there are a few notable sights downtown.

The city's crown jewel is **Lake Eola Park** (195 N. Rosalind Ave., 407/246-2827, 6 A.M.–midnight daily, free). Walking along the trail that circumnavigates it is a pleasant way to while away an afternoon, but only once you've paddled out to the middle of the lake on one of the swan-shaped boats that are available for rent can you truly say that you've experienced Lake Eola.

History buffs should explore the **Orange County Regional History Center** (65 E. Central Blvd., 407/836-8500, www.thehistorycenter.org, 10 A.M.–5 P.M. Mon.–Sat., noon–5 P.M. Sun., $9 adults, $7 seniors, $6 children, children 4 and under free), located in a 1927 building that used to be the courthouse. Three floors of immersive and well-curated permanent exhibits are heavy on 19th- and early-20th-century artifacts; although some of the museum's better material—particularly its Kerouac and Highwaymen exhibits—occasionally travel to other museums, this is still one of the better Florida-centric museums in the state.

Loch Haven Park

Located five minutes or so from downtown, **Loch Haven Park** (900 E. Princeton St., 407/246-2287, 5 A.M.–sunset daily) is a far more rewarding destination, housing museums, theaters, and a science center on its expansive grounds.

The **Mennello Museum of American Folk Art** (407/246-4278, www.mennellomuseum.org, 10:30 A.M.–4:30 P.M. Tues.–Sat., noon–4:30 P.M. Sun., $4 adults, $3 seniors, $1 students, children under 12 free) is housed in a beautiful, lakefront mansion. Founded in 1998 primarily as an exhibition space for a clutch of Earl Cunningham paintings donated by local philanthropist Marilyn Mennello, the museum diligently strives to give folk artists the respect they deserve. Cunningham's works still form the centerpiece of the Mennello, but a wide variety of visiting exhibits make it an essential stop for fans of somewhat nontraditional art.

The **Orlando Museum of Art** (407/896-4231, www.omart.org, 10 A.M.–4 P.M. Tues.–Fri., noon–4 P.M. Sat.–Sun., $8 adults, $7 seniors, students, and military, $5 children 4-17, children 3 and under free) features a respectable collection of pre-Colombian artifacts and American artwork by the likes of John Singer Sargent and Georgia O'Keeffe. OMA's African art exhibit is truly remarkable, presenting as artwork an array of fabrics, beadwork, masks, and other items that many museums would treat as anthropological items.

After gawking at folk art and artifacts for a while, the kids in your posse will likely be tugging your arm, begging for a foray to the **Orlando Science Center** (407/514-2000, www.osc.org, 10 A.M.–6 P.M. Sun.–Fri., 10 A.M.–9 P.M. Sat., $17 adults, $16 seniors and students, $12 youth, children 2 and under free). Like many such interactive museums, the exhibits at OSC are part hands-on fun, part subtle science lesson. The NatureWorks area is the most unique, with the complexities of various Florida ecosystems explained and illustrated, often with live animals. (Yes, those are alligators.) Other exhibits dedicated to dinosaurs and fun demonstrations of scientific principles, as well as the IMAX theater and planetarium, will be familiar to anyone who has visited other kid-centric science museums.

ViMi District

This burgeoning district has yet to settle on a proper designation for itself, but basically it's what's in and around Mills Avenue between Virginia Avenue at the north end and Colonial Drive at the south end. Virginia + Mills = ViMi. The area includes the Little Vietnam agglomeration of Vietnamese shops and restaurants at the southern end as well as the bars, restaurants, and galleries along the Mills Avenue corridor.

The main sight in this area is the **Harry P. Leu Gardens** (1920 N. Forest Ave., 407/246-2620, www.leugardens.org, 9 A.M.–5 P.M. daily, $7 adults, $2 children, free 9 A.M.–noon Mon.), although its Forest Avenue address puts it a block or so north of the end of Virginia

Avenue. The beautiful gardens house the largest formal rose garden in Florida as well as the largest camellia collection outside of California; backyard green-thumbs can mine the three "idea gardens" for inspiration, while the less horticulturally inclined can simply enjoy the pastoral scenery the 50 acres offer.

WINTER PARK AND MAITLAND

These two communities on the northern outskirts of Orlando are located right next to one another, and both offer their own bit of Old Florida charm. Maitland is actually one of the oldest incorporated communities in Florida, but much of its history has been overtaken by its growth as a bedroom community. The town's "cultural corridor" gives a glimpse of its foundation and personality. Winter Park, established as a planned community for wintering members of the New England elite, has been far more fastidious about maintaining its history. Its thick canopy of oak trees hangs over brick-lined streets, hiding expansive mansions and the upscale shopping and dining of its downtown area. Many visitors to Winter Park choose to drive in and walk around the Park Avenue area and then stop in some of the nearby museums and art galleries. However, a fun way to get a peek at some of the town's historic homes and beautiful scenery is the **Scenic Boat Tour** (312 E. Morse Blvd., 407/644-4056, www.scenicboattours.com, 10 A.M.–4 P.M. daily, $10 adults, $5 children, children under 2 free), which takes passengers out onto the chain of lakes that wend through the city, offering a backstage view of the truly impressive residences that line them.

◖ Downtown Winter Park

A visit to downtown Winter Park almost always begins in the areas around **Park Avenue.** This brick-paved tree-lined street is lined with an array of high-end and not-so-high-end shops and eateries, but even if you're not looking to spend or eat, a walk down Park Avenue takes you through the heart of this little urban village for some great browsing and

Central Park in downtown Winter Park

people-watching opportunities. If you're driving, take an hour or so to wander around the luxurious and historic neighborhoods immediately surrounding Park Avenue; if the price tags in the shops didn't seem expensive, some of these elegant and architecturally rich mansions certainly will. The 11-acre **Central Park** runs along Park Avenue and is home to various festivals and local events. Even if there's nothing going on, the fountains and majestic oak trees are practically begging you to spread out a blanket and have a picnic.

At the northern end of Park Avenue is the **Charles Hosmer Morse Museum of American Art** (445 N. Park Ave., 407/645-5311, www.morsemusuem.org, 9:30 A.M.–4 P.M. Tues.–Sat., 1–4 P.M. Sun., $3 adults, $1 students, children under 12 free; free 4–8 P.M. Fri. Nov.–Apr.), best known as the home of the world's most comprehensive collection of works by Louis Comfort Tiffany; everything from Tiffany lamps and stained-glass windows to pottery and paintings is on display. The Morse extends its purview beyond Tiffany to include a number of other late-19th and early-20th-century decorative pieces, art pottery, and a number of paintings and prints by the likes of Mary Cassatt, John Singer Sargent, Maxfield Parrish, Edward Hopper, and more.

A few blocks west of Park Avenue is **Hannibal Square,** a historically African American neighborhood that has slowly seen its original residents replaced by boutiques and restaurants. While there's a nice commemorative marker at the corner of New England and Pennsylvania Avenues denoting the area's cultural history, the best way to get a sense of the neighborhood's past is to pay a visit to the **Hannibal Square Heritage Center** (642 W. New England Ave., noon–4 P.M. Tues.–Thurs., noon–5 P.M. Fri., 10 A.M.–5 P.M. Sat., 10 A.M.–2 P.M. Sun., free).

The area in and around the campus of **Rollins College** is well worth a visit. Located lakeside in the heart of the picturesque campus, the **Cornell Fine Arts Museum** (1000 Holt Ave., 407/646-2526, www.rollins.edu/cfam, 10 A.M.–4 P.M. Tues.–Fri., noon–5 P.M.

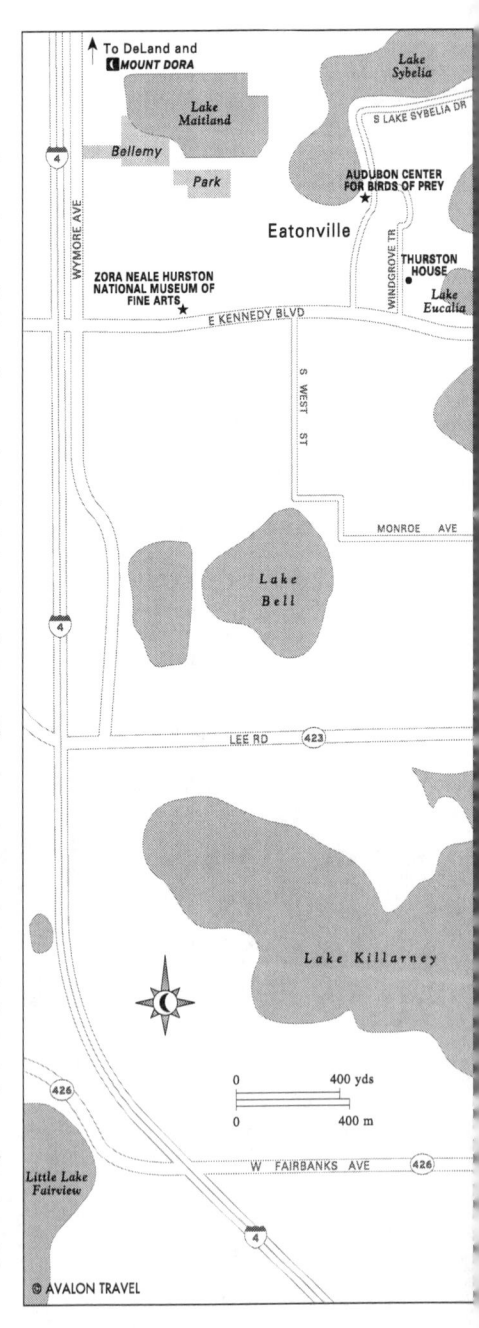

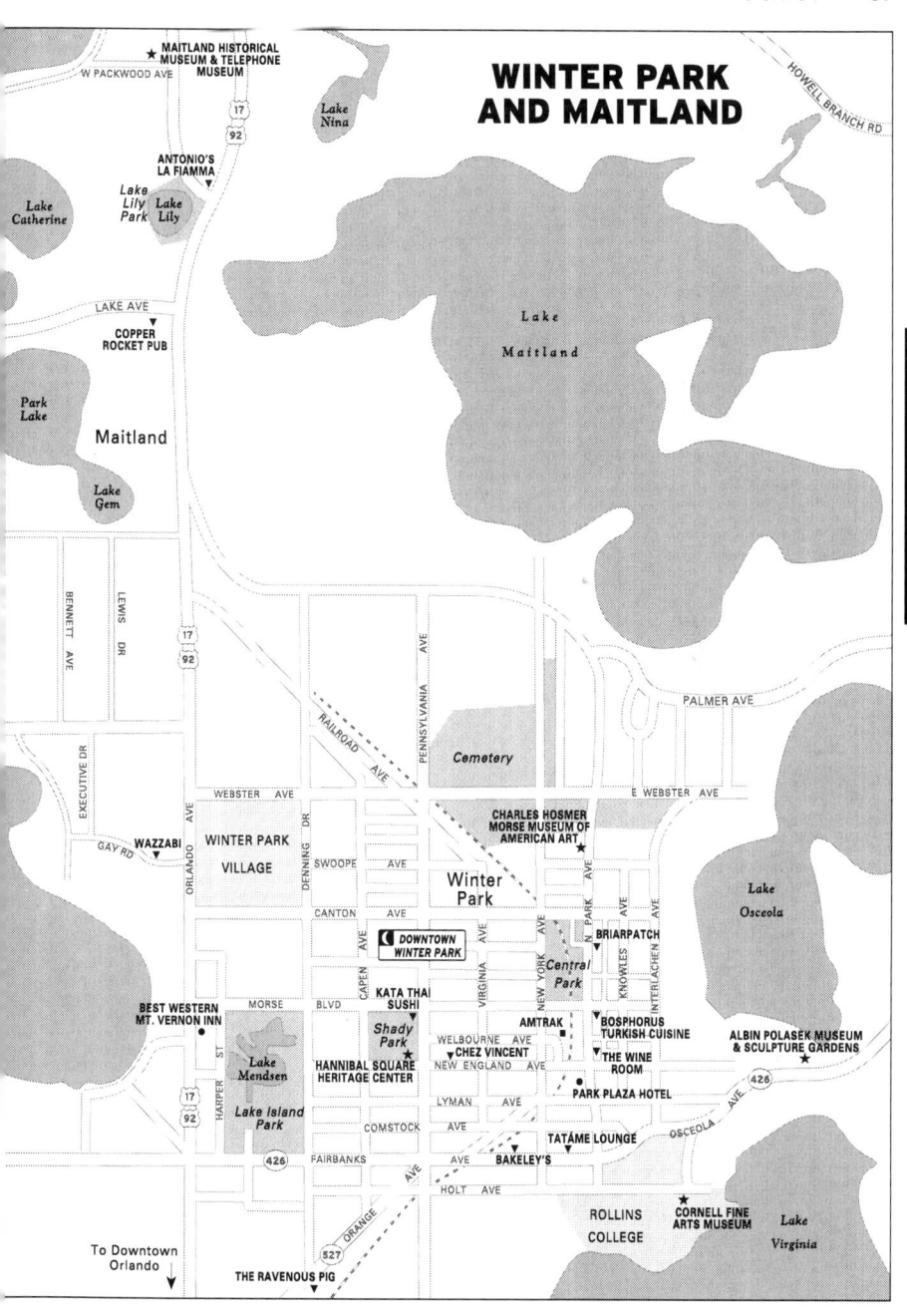

WINTER PARK AND MAITLAND

ZORA NEALE HURSTON AND EATONVILLE

The small town of Eatonville – located between Winter Park and Maitland – doesn't seem like much at first sight, but it was one of the first towns established after the Emancipation Proclamation to be a primarily African American city. Ironically enough, the town took its name not from one of its original African American leaders but from Josiah Eaton, the white landowner who sold the land that became the town.

That founding was described in Zora Neale Hurston's book *Their Eyes Were Watching God*, in which the protagonist – Janie Crawford – tells the story of her life growing up in early-20th-century Florida, a perspective that Hurston had quite a bit of authority on; she grew up in Eatonville. Every year the community pays tribute to its most famous former resident with the **ZORA! Festival** (late Jan.), dedicated not just to Hurston's work but also to a wide spectrum of African American art, culture, and music. Additionally, the small **Zora Neale Hurston National Museum of Fine Arts** (227 E. Kennedy Blvd., Eatonville, 407/647-3307, 9 A.M.-5 P.M. Mon.-Fri., donations accepted) features a couple of exhibits focused on Hurston's work and Eatonville history.

Sat.–Sun., $5 adults) houses a fantastic permanent collection, with an emphasis on classical European and American art, including a handful of paintings from the Italian Renaissance and a number of 16th- and 17th-century portraits.

Also nearby is the **Albin Polasek Museum & Sculpture Gardens** (633 Osceola Ave., 407/647-6294, www.polasek.org, gardens, galleries, residence, chapel 10 A.M.–4 P.M. Tues.–Sat., 1–4 P.M. Sun. Sept. 1–June 30; gardens only 10 A.M.–4 P.M. Mon.–Fri. July 1–Aug. 31; $5 adults, $4 seniors, $3 students, children 11 and under free, garden free). More than half of the works created by the Czech American sculptor are on display here, and the beautiful expansive gardens are a near-perfect setting for these expressive sculptures. Polasek's small but emotionally intense *The 12th Station of the Cross*, however, is not at the Museum; it can be found at his grave site at **Palm Cemetery** (1005 N. New York Ave.).

Maitland "Cultural Corridor"

Downtown Maitland doesn't have the same level of charm as downtown Winter Park, but the area known as the "Cultural Corridor" can lay claim to two highly unique museums. The **Maitland Historical Museum and Telephone Museum** (221 W. Packwood Ave., 407/644-1364, www.maitlandhistory.org, noon–4 P.M. Wed.–Sun., $3 adults, $2 children, children 5 and under free), focuses on the history of the Maitland area with lots of photographs and historical documents as well as, oddly enough, on the history of the telephone. Actually, the specific focus is on the founding of the Winter Park Telephone Company, which you'll be reminded actually happened in Maitland, along with a cluttered room filled with ancient telephone switchboards, phone booths, and other telephone-related detritus. This odd little museum is certainly not enough to build a day around, but it's a nice stop.

The nearby **Lake Lily Park** (701 Lake Lily Dr.) is home to the equally quirky **Waterhouse Residence Museum and Carpentry Shop Museum** (407/644-2451, www.maitlandhistory.org, noon–4 P.M. Wed.–Sun., $3 adults, $2 children, children 5 and under free). The Victorian-era home of builder William Waterhouse provides a snapshot look at life in the late 19th century, complete with the collection of hand-powered tools in the shed out back...otherwise known as the Carpentry Shop Museum.

Audubon Center for Birds of Prey

The **Audubon Center for Birds of Prey** (1101 Audubon Way, Maitland, 407/644-0190, www.audubonofflorida.org, 10 A.M.–4 P.M.

Tues.–Sun., $5 adults, $4 children, children under 3 free) is primarily a rehabilitative center for eagles, owls, hawks, and other raptors, but it's open to the public and offers occasional educational programs. The center rescues nearly 700 birds annually, with the goal of rereleasing them back into the wild; for that reason, the majority of the birds are kept away from human contact so they don't become acclimated to humans. Some, however, are so injured that they'll be living out the rest of their lives in captivity; these birds—some 20 species are represented—can be seen in a beautiful aviary, along with accompanying information about their various struggles. Guided on-site tours are available for groups (10–30 people, $100 per group) with five-day advance notice.

Entertainment and Events

◖ NIGHTLIFE

While Orlando's nightlife scene is heavily weighted toward the downtown area, there are a number of great places only a few minutes' drive from downtown that greatly expand the palette of offerings. For the most raucous action and the highest concentration of dance clubs, downtown is surely your best option, but to catch interesting live music or knock back a pint or two of hard-to-find beer, you'll want to get away from the crowds on Orange Avenue and head to some of Orlando's other nightlife spots.

Downtown Orlando

Downtown Orlando's biggest centers of nightlife gravity—in terms of body count, at least—are the bars in the **Church Street** (Church St. at S. Orange Ave.) area and **Wall Street Plaza** (Wall St. at N. Orange Ave.), both of which cater to a demographic mix of just-legal college kids and young businesspeople. Think 4-for-1 drink specials and body shots. However, as a brief glimpse at the crowds on Orange Avenue will tell you on any given night, there's much more to the downtown scene than that. With a few dozen bars and clubs scattered throughout the 10-square-block area, you're more than likely to find something to fit your taste.

For live music, the best options are **Back Booth** (37 W. Pine St., 407/999-2570, www.backbooth.com) and **The Social** (54 N. Orange Ave., 407/246-1419, www.thesocial.org), both of which regularly host Orlando's best local bands as well as touring indie, punk, and alternative bands. Back Booth also has late-night indie dance parties, and the Social's long-running "Phat 'n' Jazzy" night on Tuesdays is a haven for fans of underground hip-hop, acid jazz, and R&B.

For those intent on dancing the night away, **Tabu** (46 N. Orange Ave., 407/648-8363, www.tabunightclub.com, 6 P.M.–3 A.M. Tues. and Thurs.–Sat., 10 P.M.–3 A.M. Wed. and Sun.) is housed in a gorgeous old theater and focuses on streetwise hip-hop. **Club Firestone** (578 N. Orange Ave., 407/872-0066, www.clubatfirestone.com, 10 P.M.–3 A.M. Thurs.–Sun.) is a few blocks away from the main club area, but routinely brings in well-regarded underground techno, grime, and hip-hop DJs. If you're determined to relive the alternative '80s, the DJs at **Independent Bar** (70 N. Orange Ave., 407/839-0457, www.independentbar.net, 9 P.M.–2 A.M. Wed.–Sat., 10 P.M.–2 A.M. Sun. and Tues.) manage to weave New Wave, industrial, and synth-pop into a mix of contemporary indie hits and classic alternative.

Just looking for a drink? **Lizzy McCormack's Irish Pub** (55 N. Orange Ave., 407/426-8007, 2 P.M.–2 A.M. daily) has fantastic happy-hour specials, a great selection of microbrews, and outdoor tables that are perfect for watching the night unfold on Orange Avenue. **The Matador** (56 E. Pine St., 407/872-0844, 8 P.M.–2 A.M. Sat.–Thurs., 5 P.M.–2 A.M. Fri.) plays everything from soft-rock hits to obscure punk rock, and occasionally hosts DJs; a comfortable upstairs area has couches and chairs to relax in.

Located outside of what's normally considered downtown, **Eola Wine Company** (500 E. Central Blvd., 407/481-9100, www.eolawinecompany.com, 4 P.M.–12:30 A.M. Mon.–Wed., 4 P.M.–2 A.M. Thurs.–Fri., 2 P.M.–2 A.M. Sat., 2 P.M.–12:30 A.M. Sun.) in the nearby Thornton Park neighborhood is a pleasant alternative to the buzzing debauchery along Orange Avenue. Similarly, the **Orlando Brewing Tap Room** (1301 Atlanta Ave., 407/872-1117, www.orlandobrewing.com, 3–10 P.M. Mon.–Thurs., noon–midnight Fri.–Sat., noon–9 P.M. Sun.) is only about a mile from the action at Church Street, but the relaxed atmosphere, semi-industrial location and occasional live music combine with the brewery's selection of organic beers to make it feel like a world away.

ViMi and Baldwin Park Area

Still centrally located but well away from the downtown hordes is **Will's Pub** (1040 N. Mills Ave., 407/898-5070, 2 P.M.–2 A.M. daily). Will's is an Orlando institution and something of a home away from home for most of the city's musicians, thanks to its expansive and inexpensive beer selection and the wide variety of top-shelf rock and punk bands that play here. The current location is new and is neatly subdivided into three rooms: a bar, a pool and game room, and a music room, so casual patrons can enjoy a pint without having to shout over the din of the music.

The Peacock Room (1321 N. Mills Ave., 407/228-0048, www.thepeacockroom.com, 4:30 P.M.–2 A.M. Mon.–Fri., 8 P.M.–2 A.M. Sat.–Sun.) specializes in inventive martinis and lethally effective cocktails. It also doubles as one of Orlando's best hidden art galleries, with works by local artists adorning nearly all the wall space. Music is quite literally a crapshoot here; although it is almost always of high quality, any given night could bring avant-garde electronica, rowdy punk rock, a singer-songwriter, or an indie band. Not to worry, though: If the current act is not your thing, the music room is quite separate from the bar area.

Orlando beer fans celebrated when **Redlight Redlight** (745 Bennett Rd., 407/893-9832, 7 P.M.–2 A.M. Mon.–Sat.) moved from its original location in Winter Park's Hannibal Square area, as local restrictions forced the bar to close far too early. Now, with its new late-night hours, hop-heads are able to indulge themselves with Redlight's exceedingly well-curated selection of microbrews and imports. Cask ales and small-batch craft beers are the specialties, and thankfully the bartenders are as helpful as they are knowledgeable. There are three things to remember about this place: no Bud or Miller products, no smoking, and no credit cards are accepted.

Winter Park and Maitland

While downtown Winter Park isn't exactly known for its raucous after-hours scene, there are a couple of interesting places. **The Wine Room** (270 Park Ave. S., Winter Park, 407/696-9463, www.thewineroomonline.com, 10 A.M.–10 P.M. Mon.–Thurs., 10 A.M.–midnight Fri.–Sat., noon–7 P.M. Sun.) utilizes the Enomatic wine-dispensing system, meaning patrons can indulge themselves in over 100 different wines—one ounce at a time. Of course, an extensive selection of full bottles is available, ranging in price from reasonable to ridiculous. A handful of imported beers are also available on tap, and a well-stocked cheese case is staffed by folks knowledgeable about pairings.

Tatáme Lounge (223 W. Fairbanks Ave., Winter Park, 407/628-2408, www.tatamelounge.com, 5 P.M.–1 A.M. Mon.–Thurs., 5 P.M.–2 A.M. Fri.–Sat.) caters to the Rollins College crowd, but it's far from your typical college bar. In fact, it's not really a bar at all. Guests sip premium sake or boba tea while local musicians—typically adventurous DJs or acoustic artists—perform. The dimly lit environs are mellow and modern, but the crowd is boisterous and chatty.

The **Copper Rocket Pub** (106 Lake Ave., Maitland, 407/645-0069, www.copperrocketpub.com, 2 P.M.–2 A.M. daily) is situated in a Maitland strip mall, but inside it feels like a well-worn roadhouse. Billiard balls click around on a single pool table, and a tiny stage hosts an array of Orlando bands playing everything from rockabilly and country to punk and soul music. The pub grub here is basic, but the beer list is extensive.

THE ARTS

Nobody will mistake Orlando's art scene for New York City's or even Miami's, but marquee performing arts groups like the Orlando Opera, Orlando Ballet, Orlando Philharmonic, and a slew of smaller grassroots arts organizations maintain a cultural scene that's growing and vibrant. Arts-conscious travelers will want to avail themselves of the **Orlando Arts Getaways** (407/872-2382, www.redchairproject.com) put together by the city's Arts & Cultural Alliance. These vacation packages provide discount rates on admission to cultural performances as well as hotel and restaurant bookings.

Galleries

There is no central arts district in Orlando, and the closest you'll come is the area near the intersection of Mills Avenue and Virginia Drive known colloquially as the ViMi district. There you can find a small handful of art spaces and galleries, including the superlative **Comma Gallery** (813 Virginia Dr., 407/376-1400, 11 A.M.–4 P.M. Tues.–Sat., free), which is frequently the site of some of the city's most interesting contemporary art exhibitions.

Downtown, the **City Arts Factory** (29 S. Orange Ave., 407/648-7060, www.cityartsfactory.com, 11 A.M.–7 P.M. Mon.–Sat., free) struggles to provide a dose of culture for an area of town that's all business during the day and all partying at night. This multiroom facility has a bit of a rock-and-roll feel to it (amplified by a music space upstairs), and is quickly becoming one of the most prestigious places in Orlando for young, daring artists to exhibit their work.

Theater

Located downtown in a beautiful performance space, the **Mad Cow Theatre Company** (105 S. Magnolia Ave., 407/297-8788, www.madcowtheatre.com) can't quite decide if it wants to be an edgy, urban theater or a crowd-pleasing night out for the blue-hair set. Production schedules have featured everything from Pinter and Chekhov to *The Glass Menagerie* and *The Fantasticks*.

Theatre Downtown (2113 N. Orange Ave., 407/841-0083, www.theatredowntown.net) isn't actually downtown but a couple of miles north near Loch Haven Park. The fare here is usually just a step or two above community theater in terms of the repertory work performed, but the casts, sets, and direction are almost always top-notch.

Orlando Shakespeare Theater (812 E. Rollins St., 407/447-1700, www.orlandoshakes.org) is situated in beautiful Loch Haven Park, and in addition to the expected slate of works by the Bard, which are almost always produced in unexpected ways, the Shakes puts on small-scale Broadway musicals and family-friendly fare.

Movies

The best place in town to catch a flick is definitely the **Enzian Theater** (1300 S. Orlando Ave., Maitland, 407/629-0054, www.enzian.org). The Enzian serves up art house and international fare on screen and has comfortable chairs and table service from a top-notch and inventive kitchen: think mean roasted wild-mushroom salads or pizza Margherita instead of popcorn and nachos, and beer and wine instead of watered-down sodas. The Enzian's chalet-like building and its tree-canopied grounds are thoroughly romantic, and its recently opened Eden Bar now allows film fans to grab a cocktail before the movie starts.

Considerably less fancy, and less centrally located, the **Touchstar Cinemas – Southchase 7** (12441 S. Orange Blossom Tr., 407/888-2025, www.dattanientertainment.com) is little more than another budget-conscious multiplex in a strip mall. However, for fans of the splashy Indian cinema spectacle known as Bollywood, the Southchase is the only game in town. There's almost always at least one first-run Indian film here, slotted in among current

Hollywood blockbusters; if the Bollywood film has enough hype behind it, the theater even sells Samosas in the lobby.

FESTIVALS

The **Florida Film Festival** (late Mar., www.floridafilmfestival.com) happens at the Enzian Theater, and is one of the premier film festivals in the Southeast. The 10-day event not only features a superlative slate of independent and international movies, many of which have their national or regional premieres here, but also has high-profile actors and directors as guests. The FFF recently added a food and wine component, bringing celebrity chefs (2007 featured Anthony Bourdain) and many local restaurants to the table for tastings and unique gastronomic tours of the area.

Downtown Orlando is besieged by hundreds of musicians and music-biz types during the three-day **Florida Music Festival** (mid-May, www.floridamusicfestival.com). A few well-known acts are interspersed throughout the lineup, which primarily focuses on local and regional bands looking for their shot at the big time.

For years, the **Orlando International Fringe Theatre Festival** (mid-May, www.orlandofringe.org) stuck to the format utilized by the original Fringe in Edinburgh; dozens of empty storefronts and other spaces in downtown Orlando were turned into ad hoc theater venues, where an array of out-of-the-mainstream works could be presented in a playful and slightly competitive environment. Today, the Orlando Fringe retains its dedication to challenging or unusual theater pieces, but the whole affair has been moved to the area in and around Loch Haven Park, mainly utilizing the multiple established theater spaces there. While this circumscribed geography cuts down on the sense of exploration, it has actually made the 12 days of the festival much easier to navigate, allowing both the curious and hardcore theater fans easier access to these interesting works.

It started in 1991 as a form of loosely organized awareness-raising with gay and lesbian folks being encouraged to "wear red and be seen" at Walt Disney World on the first Saturday in June. Today, the annual **Gay Days** (early June, www.gaydays.com) celebrations last more than a week, bringing nearly 150,000 LGBT and LGBT-friendly visitors to the city. Events both official and unofficial have popped up throughout the city, few of which have anything to do with the ritual red-shirt visit to the Magic Kingdom. From a convention-like Expo and organized visits to the other Disney parks to comedy shows and all-night dance parties, Gay Days has become an integral part of Orlando's annual events calendar.

Shopping

ORLANDO

There's little shopping in downtown Orlando proper, but **Etoile Boutique** (2424 E. Robinson St., 407/895-6363, www.etoileboutique.net, noon–8 P.M. Mon.–Sat., noon–5 P.M. Sun.)—located in the nascent Milk District, a mile or so from downtown—is an essential stop for shoppers interested in locally-designed clothes and crafts. Hip, modern, and defiantly pro-Orlando, Etoile features everything from unique soaps and candles to handmade bags, clothes, and vintage gear.

A mile or so on the other side of downtown, situated along Lake Ivanhoe, is Orlando's **Antique District**. While there is only about a block of actual antiques stores, the district extends another block or so to include unique shops like the vintage vinyl of **Rock & Roll Heaven** (1814 N. Orange Ave., 407/896-1952, www.rock-n-roll-heaven.com, 10 A.M.–7:30 P.M. Mon.–Sat., 11 A.M.–4 P.M. Sun.) and the vintage clothing of **Sequel Fine Clothing Traders** (1616 N. Orange Ave., 407/895-7447, 11 A.M.–6 P.M. Mon.–Sat.). **Tim's Wine**

OURLANDO VERSUS BUY LOCAL ORLANDO

In these days when "shop local" is a mantra among right-minded folks, it may seem strange to have two entities battling over which is more local, but that's just what has happened in Orlando. In early 2008 the owner of a local café and the director of a progressive nonprofit started a website – www.ourlando.com – intended to highlight the offerings of independent locally owned businesses. Ourlando charges businesses a few hundred dollars per year to be members, and in return they get marketing and advertising avenues developed to promote their businesses.

In January 2009 the City of Orlando launched its Buy Local Orlando project, which grants a $99 membership to any business that pays city taxes, and offers a directory, window decals, and a consultation with the Disney Entrepreneur Center. It may sound great to have two organizations promoting local businesses, but not quite: The city's program allows any business – whether it's a mom-and-pop shoe store or a big-box chain – to claim to be "local." While these municipally-run programs are common throughout the country, Orlando's is one of the only ones that allows chain stores to promote themselves as local businesses, a fact that brought withering criticism both from Orlando's "locals first" community and from bigger cities like Austin, who run similar programs without the chain-store allowance. Community-minded shoppers should be advised that just because a business boasts a "Buy Local Orlando" sticker in its window, it may not be quite as local as you think.

Market (1223 N. Orange Ave., 407/895-9463, www.timswine.blogspot.com, 10 A.M.–7 P.M. Mon.–Fri., 10 A.M.–5 P.M. Sat.) is a friendly and knowledgeable spot to pick up a singular bottle of wine, while **Kismet** (1808 N. Orange Ave., 407/894-8905, 11 A.M.–8 P.M. Mon.–Thurs., 11 A.M.–9 P.M. Fri.–Sat., noon–4 P.M. Sun.) is part local-centric art gallery, part jewelry shop.

WINTER PARK

Shopping is the activity of choice along Winter Park's **Park Avenue,** and it's hard to deny the appeal of spending an afternoon browsing the windows along this tree-lined street. Though populated with a few well-known stores like Pottery Barn, Williams Sonoma, and the Gap, the real draws on Park Avenue are the local boutiques like **Bullfish** (102 N. Park Ave., 407/644-2969, www.bullfishparkavenue.com, 10 A.M.–7 P.M. Mon.–Sat., noon–5 P.M. Sun.), which is—honest to God—a combination wine shop and hand-baked pet-treat store. **Tuni's** (301 S. Park Ave., 407/628-1609, 10 A.M.–7 P.M. Mon.–Sat., noon–6 P.M. Sun.) specializes in trendy, exclusive, and expensive women's clothing; they also have a selection of accessories and local jewelry. **Kathmandu** (352 N. Park Ave., 407/647-7071, www.tribalasia.com, 11 A.M.–8 P.M. Mon.–Sat., noon–6 P.M. Sun.), on the other hand, specializes in hippy-infused threads and knickknacks.

A few blocks away from Park Avenue in the Hannibal Square area there is a handful of clothing and jewelry boutiques; the most unique is **The Baraka Collection** (444 W. New England Ave., 407/260-1400, www.barakacollection.com), a gallery-cum-shop focused on contemporary Middle Eastern and Arabic art and furnishings.

Nearby **Winter Park Village** (510 N. Orlando Ave.) is an open-air shopping mall, with the usual suspects like Pier 1 and Barnes & Noble nestled alongside a few nice local boutiques; there's also a movie theater and several restaurants.

MALL AT MILLENIA

With outlets for Tiffany, Coach, Nordstrom, Burberry, Chanel, and more, the annoyingly misspelled **Mall at Millenia** (4200 Conroy Rd.,

10 A.M.–9 P.M. Mon.–Sat., noon–7 P.M. Sun.) considers itself "Orlando's destination for luxury brand shopping." And while it certainly is that, it also draws a number of tourists from the nearby theme parks who may just want to get a good deal on some American sneakers at the Vans Store or pick up a new iPod at the gleaming Apple Store.

Sports and Recreation

PARKS

Florida is blessed with an abundance of beautiful and pastoral springs, those places where water bubbles up from the earth to feed rivers and providing sustenance. At **Wekiva Springs State Park** (1800 Wekiwa Circle, Apopka, 407/884-2008, www.floridasateparks.org/wekiwasprings, 8 A.M.–sunset daily, $5 vehicles with 2–8 people, $3 single-occupant vehicles), *pastoral* isn't the first word that comes to mind. The year-round 72-degree water means there's almost always a crowd relaxing on the sloping banks and splashing around in the large water basin, making it feel more like a municipal swimming pool than the remarkable natural gift that it is. Nonetheless, beyond the main swimming area there are ample boating opportunities as the spring water flows into the Wekiva River, as well as well-marked hiking trails and numerous primitive, RV, and family campsites.

Kelly Park at Rock Springs (400 E. Kelly Park Rd., Apopka, 407/889-4179, 9 A.M.–7 P.M. daily, $1, children under 5 free) has no pool-like area, as the springs immediately begin flowing into a briskly moving stream that proves irresistible to folks who want to go tubing. There are a number of tube-rental outfits near the park's entrance, most of which offer tubes for $3–5.

the swimming area at Wekiva Springs State Park

The more centrally located **Gaston Edwards Park** (1236 N. Orange Ave., Orlando, 407/246-2283, 5 A.M.–sunset daily) is on Lake Ivanhoe near downtown; the preferred activities here are Jet-Skiing and waterskiing. Landlubbers typically stay onshore to enjoy a game of volleyball.

SPECTATOR SPORTS

The National Basketball Association's **Orlando Magic** (www.nba.com/magic) will play their final season at the current **Amway Arena** (600 W. Amelia St.) in 2009–2010; after that, the team—and the arena's name—will move to a new facility called the **Orlando Events Center,** located just a few blocks away. The city's Arena Football League team, the two-time Arena Bowl champion **Orlando Predators,** and the National Indoor Soccer League's **Orlando Sharks** also play in the Amway Arena and will be moving to the new location as well.

The seen-better-days **Florida Citrus Bowl** (1610 W. Church St.) is used for occasional marquee events, most notably the **Florida Classic,** a football showdown between two historically-black colleges, Bethune-Cookman University and Florida A&M; the Classic brings tens of thousands of football fans to town in November for the game and, more notably, the legendary halftime show. The Citrus Bowl stadium also hosts the **Capital One Bowl** (formerly the Tangerine Bowl, then the Citrus Bowl; the New Year's Day game pits the Southeastern Conference against the Atlantic Coast Conference) and, a few days earlier, the **Champs Sports Bowl** (Atlantic Coast Conference and Big Ten teams). The aging facility is scheduled for a $175 million renovation in 2010.

The **Arnold Palmer Invitational** golf meet is held at the Palmer-owned **Bay Hill Club and Lodge** (9000 Bay Hill Blvd.); the tournament is held in late March, usually just a couple of weeks before the Masters, and most of the PGA's top golfers show up to play.

For something a little more fast-moving, **Orlando Speed World** (19164 E. Colonial Dr., 407/568-1367, www.orlandospeedworld.org) has stock-car races, pickup-truck races, demolition derbies, and stunt shows nearly year-round; it's the Thanksgiving weekend "Crash-A-Rama," though, that brings out the big crowds for some truly riotous school bus—yes, school bus—races.

GOLF

The city-owned **Dubsdread** (549 W. Par St., 407/246-2551, www.golfdubsdread.com, from $27) was originally designed in 1923, and it wears its history proudly. The relatively short par-72 course isn't all that challenging, but the sloping greens and water features are picturesque; the Tap Room restaurant is a local favorite among golfers and non-golfers alike.

Winter Pines Golf Course (950 S. Ranger Blvd., Winter Park, 407/671-3172, from $15) is a small par-67 course located in a tidy Winter Park neighborhood and is routinely rated as one of the best golf values in Central Florida.

WATER SPORTS

The chain of lakes that dot Orlando's landscape means that the area is a prime location for wakeboarding and waterskiing. **Orlando Watersports Complex** (8615 Florida Rock Rd., 407/251-3100, www.orlandowatersports.com, 11 A.M.–sunset Mon.–Fri., 10 A.M.–sunset Sat.–Sun.) takes full advantage of that, with two lakes dedicated to high-speed water activities. A series of cables runs above each lake, allowing boarders, wake-skaters, and waterskiers to careen along at top velocity, jumping ramps and practicing their tricks at either 18 mph in the beginners lake or at 20 mph in the advanced one; ski boats also run on the lakes. There's a pro shop and a snack bar, and lessons and rentals are available.

Accommodations

ORLANDO
$50-100
Located in a residential neighborhood, the **Veranda Bed & Breakfast Inn** (707 E. Washington St., 407/849-0321, www.theverandabandb.com, from $99 d) is spread out across four buildings, but with only 10 guest rooms, it never comes close to feeling like a hotel. Several of the guest rooms have private entrances, and the two guest rooms in the Keylime Cottage can be combined to make a two-bedroom two-bath home away from home, complete with a full kitchen. The spacious grounds include a quiet courtyard and swimming pool, and all of the guest rooms have private baths and televisions.

$100-150
The **Courtyard at Lake Lucerne** (211 N. Lucerne Circle E., 407/648-5188, www.orlandohistoricinn.com, from $125 d) is another four-building accommodation set in a residential neighborhood. More traditional bed-and-breakfast-type guest rooms can be found among three beautifully restored early-20th-century buildings, but it's the 15 stylish one-bedroom suites of the art deco Wellborn Suites building that set the Courtyard apart; though aimed at extended-stay business travelers (with desks, kitchenettes, and Wi-Fi), they're comfortable enough for anyone planning a stay in the area of more than a day or so.

Overlooking Lake Eola and downtown Orlando, the **Eo Inn & Urban Spa** (227 N. Eola Dr., 407/481-8485, www.eoinn.com, from $129 d) is a modern European-style boutique hotel aimed directly at luxury travelers, but the rates are surprisingly affordable. The 17 guest rooms are Wi-Fi equipped and decked out with contemporary furnishings and supersoft beds with down comforters. With its relaxing rooftop Jacuzzi and a heavy emphasis on the various spa treatments available on-site, the Eo achieves a level of intimacy that's somewhat incongruous with its close proximity to downtown.

Over $200
Formerly an extraluxurious outpost of the Westin chain, the **Grand Bohemian** (325 S. Orange Ave., 407/313-9000, www.grandbohemianhotel.com, from $209 d) is now operated by the boutique-minded Kessler Collection (also the operators of the Casa Monica in St. Augustine). With its 250 guest rooms spread over 15 floors in the heart of downtown, *boutique* isn't quite the adjective I would use to describe the Grand Bohemian, but there's a level of privacy and personal service here that's completely unmatched by other local hotels of this size. From the dark wood furnishings and decadent velvet drapes to the same sort of soft beds that made the Westin famous, much of the luxury of the hotel's former incarnation is intact. The bohemian vibe is maintained with an understated emphasis on art (there's a curated gallery), plus the downstairs Bosendorfer Lounge features tasteful live music nightly, and the award-winning Bohème restaurant is best known for its Sunday jazz brunch.

WINTER PARK AND MAITLAND
$100-150
A Best Western may not be the sort of lodging one would expect in an upper-crust village like Winter Park, and accordingly the **Best Western Mt. Vernon Inn** (110 S. Orlando Ave., Winter Park, 407/647-1166, from $135 d) isn't your typical Best Western. Essentially a motel with guest rooms that face a parking lot, the guest rooms are clean, quiet, and exceedingly well-maintained, if not of the most recent vintage. Make sure that you pop into the on-site Red Fox Lounge for a drink and a listen to the *Saturday Night Live*–like husband-and-wife musical team Mark and Lorna.

$150-200
Much more in keeping with Winter Park's character is the **Park Plaza Hotel** (307 S. Park Ave., Winter Park, 407/647-1072,

www.parkplazahotel.com, from $179 d), a 28-room "vintage boutique" hotel that overlooks all the activity on bustling Park Avenue and commands a price (and weekend waiting list) commensurate with its location. Brick-faced walls and antique furnishings give the tiny guest rooms at the Park Plaza a rustic lived-in feel, but the exceptional service and charming atmosphere evoke a sense of long-lost luxury.

The **Thurston House** (851 Lake Ave., Maitland, 407/539-1911, www.thurstonhouse.com, from $190 d) is an 1885 Queen Anne–style farmhouse set on a beautifully landscaped lot. There are only three guest rooms, all of which have free Wi-Fi, flat screen televisions and DVD players, and private baths; the best is the O'Heir Room, which has a fireplace, a sleigh bed, and an enormous bay window looking out onto Lake Eulalia.

Food

Central Orlando and the Winter Park area are blessed with a number of excellent restaurants. However, Orlando's "Restaurant Row"—home to a high concentration of upscale and mid-scale restaurants—is located in the tourist district along Sand Lake Road, near Walt Disney World and the other Orlando theme parks, International Drive, and the Orange County Convention Center.

ORLANDO
Breakfast and Light Bites
Downtown, the **Breakfast Club** (63 E. Pine St., 407/843-1559, 7 A.M.–2:30 P.M. daily, main courses from $4) is one of a handful of eggs-and-bacon joints. Its central location and no-frills atmosphere means it caters primarily to office workers, but the food here is decent and incredibly inexpensive.

The main focus at ◖ **Pom-Pom's Teahouse & Sandwicheria** (67 N. Bumby Ave., 407/894-0865, 11 A.M.–8 P.M. Mon.–Thurs., 24 hours Fri.–Sat., closes at 6 P.M. Sun., main courses from $7) is sandwiches and tea. More than two dozen varieties of hot and iced teas are available, and the array of pressed sandwiches ranges from tuna melts and Dagwoods to various combinations of meats, cheeses, chutneys, fruits, vegetables, Asian slaw, and more. Breakfast is only served on the weekends, when the restaurant is open for marathon 24-hour sessions catering to the late-night and early morning crowds; egg-and-cheese sandwiches, potatoes napoleon, crepes, and the standards of grits, bacon, and toast are available then. Owner Pom Moongauklang applies her quirky style to everything on the menu, resulting in a personality-filled restaurant that's a perennial favorite with locals.

Ba Le (1227 N. Mills Ave., 407/898-8011, 9:30 A.M.–8 P.M. Mon.–Sat., main courses from $3) is a Vietnamese restaurant–French bakery–sandwich shop that got its start as a franchise chain in Hawaii. While there aren't many chains listed in this guide, I felt the need to bring this one to your attention because the fresh French bread, seasoned meat, and herbs that go into Ba Le's sandwiches are definitely worth checking out. The fact that they're super-cheap is just a bonus.

American
Crooked Bayou (50 E. Central Blvd., 407/839-5852, 11 A.M.–2 A.M. Mon.–Fri., noon–2 A.M. Sat., main courses from $8) is actually more of a bar than a restaurant, but the New Orleans–style fare, including po'boys, jambalaya, and gumbo, is consistently impressive; don't miss their tater tots and fried pickles.

The early '90s decor and vibe at **Dexter's** (808 E. Washington St., 407/648-2777, 11 A.M.–10 P.M. Mon.–Thurs., 11 A.M.–11 P.M. Fri.–Sat., 10 A.M.–10 P.M. Sun., main courses from $10) makes it feel like the wine bar from an episode of *Friends*. The menu is anything but stuck in the past, with plenty of inventive

Asian-inspired seafood dishes, decadent appetizers like watermelon carpaccio, and steaks and pasta as well as an extensive wine list.

Kres Chophouse (17 W. Church St., 407/447-7950, 11:30 A.M.–midnight Mon.–Fri., 5 P.M.–midnight Sat., main courses from $20) is situated smack-dab among the bars and clubs of Church Street, but the atmosphere here celebrates an entirely different sort of decadence. The Kobe beef, chateaubriand, and lobster tails are served in a sumptuous modern environment, with prices to match.

Spanish and Mediterranean

A recent expansion of the Tampa institution **Ceviche** (125 W. Church St., 321/281-8140, www.ceviche.com, 11 A.M.–10 P.M. Mon., 11 A.M.–2 A.M. Tues.–Fri., 5 P.M.–2 A.M. Sat., tapas from $6, main courses from $14) in Orlando completely eschews the tiny intimate surroundings of the original restaurant for two massive noisy dining rooms. Still, the bare brick and aged-wood furnishings have a certain romantic charm. The strength of the extensive and authentically Spanish tapas menu—more than three dozen hot and cold small plates are available to choose from—isn't diminished at all by the surroundings.

Cafe Annie (131 N. Orange Ave., 407/420-4041, breakfast and lunch 7:30 A.M.–3 P.M. Mon.–Fri., dinner 5–10 P.M. Mon.–Thurs., 5 P.M.–2 A.M. Fri.–Sat., main courses from $6) suffers from something of an identity crisis. Early in the morning, steam trays full of grits, bacon, and eggs beckon office workers for breakfast, while late at night, drink specials and live music cater to the revelers on Orange Avenue. In between those times, Cafe Annie has a great menu of Greek and Mediterranean dishes. From kebabs and falafel to grape leaves and Greek salads, the basics are covered, along with harder-to-find delicacies like kibbeh, loubieh bi zayt, and Lebanese pita-bread salad.

Vegan and Vegetarian

There aren't all that many vegetarian-friendly restaurants in Orlando, but the few that do exist are truly exceptional. **Ethos Vegan Kitchen** (1235 N. Orange Ave., 407/228-3898, 11 A.M.–10 P.M. Mon.–Sat., 10 A.M.–3 P.M. Sun., main courses from $8) has a comfort-food vibe, with lots of fresh and steamed vegetables, hearty soups, and mashed potatoes that are really just a starch bowl for the decadent gravy. Entrées like "sheep's pie" and pecan-crusted eggplant are joined on the menu by pasta dishes, sandwiches, and pizza, all of which are 100 percent vegan.

Dandelion Communitea Cafe (618 N Thornton Ave., 407/362-1864, 11 A.M.–3 P.M. Mon., 11 A.M.–10 P.M. Tues.–Sat., noon–6 P.M. Sun., main courses from $8) isn't completely vegan, but it's close, and all of their sandwiches, soups, salads, and starters are vegetarian and built out of fresh fruits, vegetables, and grains. Add to that a selection of all-organic teas and a palpable commitment to the local community and ecological causes, and it would be easy to assume that the vibe in Dandelion might be preachy or didactic. In fact, the opposite is true, and the environment is both welcoming and homey; in fact, it's in a gaily painted repurposed house.

A frequent complaint of vegetarians is "fake-out food," those odd-tasting and unsatisfying dishes that purport to be meatless analogs of fleshy entrées. **Garden Cafe** (810 W. Colonial Dr., 407/999-9799, 11 A.M.–10 P.M. Tues.–Fri., noon–10 P.M. Sat.–Sun., main courses from $10) is the sort of place that should silence such complaints. The Chinese menu is completely meatless, from the pepper steak to the sesame chicken. Of course, the trick here is the exceptional sauces used by the kitchen, but hey, that's the way it is in any Chinese restaurant, right? While the atmosphere is somewhat lacking (it's in a reconstituted Pizza Hut), the succulent guilt-free dishes more than make up for such minor shortcomings and will appeal to meat-eaters and vegetarians alike.

Asian

If you're not Chinese, odds are that when you settle into your seat at the semi-fancy **Lam's Garden** (2505 E. Colonial Dr., 407/896-0370, 11 A.M.–10 P.M. daily, main courses from $9) you'll be handed a green menu and see the expected array of moo goo gai pan, fried rice, and "Imperial Jade Delight"–type dishes. But ask for a red menu and select from a more thoroughly authentic Chinese experience, with dishes like ducks' feet, steamed fish, water spinach, and more.

Orlando's Little Vietnam is home to an extraordinary number of extraordinary Vietnamese restaurants, so in all honesty, if you park your car near the intersection of Colonial Drive and Mills Avenue, you're likely to find a good Vietnamese eatery. Two of the largest and most popular are **Pho 88** (730 N. Mills Ave., 407/897-3488, 10 A.M.–10 P.M. daily, main courses from $7), which specializes in traditional meat-and-noodle soup; and **Vietnam Town** (1101 E. Colonial Dr., 407/895-9698, 11 A.M.–11 P.M. daily, main courses from $9), which is larger, somewhat fancier (bordering on tacky), and boasting a broader menu that, for those of us who don't speak Vietnamese, is helpfully illustrated with photos.

Tucked in among all the Vietnamese restaurants is **Shin Jung** (11:30 A.M.–10 P.M. Mon.–Sat., 1:30–10 P.M. Sun., main courses from $15), an excellent eatery that happens to be one of the only Korean restaurants in Orlando. Although the tables are set up so you can barbecue your own meat at the table in the traditional style, you needn't come prepared to cook; the kitchen dishes up soups and rice and noodle dishes, along with one of the best dol sot bibimbap bowls around. The atmosphere in this converted house, besides being thick with grill smoke, is friendly and comfortable, and it's almost always crowded.

WINTER PARK AND MAITLAND
Breakfast and Light Bites

Bakeley's (345 W. Fairbanks Ave., Winter Park, 407/645-5767, 7 A.M.–11 P.M. Sun.–Thurs., 7 A.M.–midnight Fri.–Sat., main courses from $6) is a family-owned diner specializing in ample breakfast platters. Enormous omelets and thick French toast are the marquee dishes, but even more "simple" dishes like the Floridian manage to pile on exponentially larger servings of eggs, multiple meats, grits, and potatoes. The "skillet" breakfasts pile it all together in a cast-iron cooker, blending the flavors in a way that no Denny's could ever hope to match. Lunch and dinner are standard diner fare with a few Greek touches.

Although they serve breakfast at the too-cute-for-words **Briarpatch** (252 N. Park Ave., Winter Park, 407/628-8651, 7 A.M.–6 P.M. Mon.–Sat., 8 A.M.–5 P.M. Sun., main courses from $7), the early-morning meals are unremarkable, as are the lunches. However, the sidewalk seating along Park Avenue is a perfect setting to enjoy some of the rich cakes and homemade ice cream.

American

◖ **The Ravenous Pig** (1234 N. Orange Ave., Winter Park, 407/628-2333, lunch 11:30 A.M.–2:30 P.M. Tues.–Sat., dinner 5:30–10 P.M. Tues.–Thurs., 5:30–11 P.M. Fri.–Sat., main courses from $14) emerged on the Winter Park dining scene in late 2007 and its gastropub concept—serving exceptionally inventive and perfectly prepared dishes in an environment that's part pub, part fine dining—has proven enormously successful. Braised pork bellies, lobster tacos, steak tartare, raw-bar offerings, blue cheese burgers, and the truly divine truffle fries are just a few of the selections that have helped cement the Pig's reputation as a culinary destination. The carefully manicured wine and beer lists and surprisingly friendly staff—not to mention the monthly pig roasts—have ensured a steady stream of regulars, so you'd be wise to call ahead for a reservation.

Asian

It's far from innovative to slot sushi onto a menu of Thai cuisine, but **Kata Thai Sushi** (610 W. Morse Blvd., Winter Park, 407/388-3729, 11 A.M.–10 P.M. Sun.–Thurs., 11 A.M.–11 P.M. Fri.–Sat., main courses from $14) does a fine job of integrating a variety of Japanese dishes and lunchtime bento boxes with their curries and chili-drenched whole snapper. During the spring and fall, the outdoor seating area is a beautiful place to enjoy your meal, but the dining room is plenty serene and tasteful for when the weather isn't cooperative.

Wazzabi (1408 Gay Rd., Winter Park, 407/647-8744, 11 A.M.–10 P.M. Sun.–Thurs., 11 A.M.–11 P.M. Fri.–Sat., main courses from $14) may not look like what most people envision when they think of authentic Japanese restaurants, but the sleek surfaces, stylish waitstaff, and progressive down-tempo soundtrack actually seem a lot more like Tokyo than many bamboo-walled kimono-clad sushi shops. All that style comes with a price, but the meals at Wazzabi are absolutely worth it. The main dining room features sushi, Japanese entrées with a few surprises like soba-wrapped pan-fried duck and hot-and-sour scallops, and steaks; a glass-walled teppanyaki room serves table-grilled food, but instead of the tiny frozen shrimp and chewy chicken on offer at most such places, Wazzabi offers lobster tail, New York strip, salmon, and even Kobe beef.

French and European

The tiny ornate dining room at **Chez Vincent** (533 W. New England Ave., Winter Park, 407/599-2929, lunch 11:30 A.M.–2 P.M. daily, dinner 6–10 P.M. daily, main courses from $15) has been a Winter Park date-night mainstay since it opened more than a decade ago, and its classic French cuisine once earned the restaurant a place on Zagat's "America's Top Restaurants" list. Yet somehow, Chez Vincent manages not to feel like a stuffy stuck-in-the-past eatery. Maybe it's due to the cozy dining area or the way the kitchen makes standards like duck à l'orange seem interesting, and the atmosphere is friendly and relaxed and the food expertly prepared.

The modern-meets-traditional, east-meets-west atmosphere of **Bosphorous Turkish Cuisine** (108 S. Park Ave., Winter Park, 407/644-8609, 11:30 A.M.–10 P.M. Sun.–Thurs., 11:30 A.M.–11 P.M. Fri.–Sat., main courses from $12) reflects many of the clichéd notions that come up whenever discussing Turkey, and sometimes when dining here you get the sense that the restaurant is run by the country's Inferiority Complex Ministry as there's so much insistence on Turkey's beauty and sophistication. When dinner arrives, it's clear that the crew at Bosphorous is much more concerned with immaculately preparing an array of dishes built around vertically grilled meat (with a typically Turkish emphasis on lamb), fresh seafood, and inventive nonwrap uses of pita bread. A variety of hot and cold appetizers are also available for those who want to taste a range of different Turkish foods.

Antonio's La Fiamma (611 S. Orlando Ave., Maitland, 407/645-1035, lunch 11:30 A.M.–2:30 P.M. Mon.–Fri., dinner 5–10 P.M. Mon.–Sat., main courses from $18) serves exquisite and extensive Italian dishes that depend heavily on the use of a wood-burning oven. So, while you may have had a veal chop or fontina-stuffed chicken breast before, it's doubtful that you've had them imbued with the rustic flavor that so many of the dishes at Antonio's have. The decadently sauced and seasoned rice and pasta dishes are also homespun and hearty. The elegant atmosphere belies the reasonable prices and friendly service.

Practicalities

INFORMATION AND SERVICES
Visitor Information
The only official visitors center in Orlando is in the heart of the tourist district. However, the city of Orlando recently introduced the **Orlando Ambassador Program,** which put an army of Segway-driving friendly faces on the streets of downtown.

Media
The daily *Orlando Sentinel* (www.orlandosentinel.com) newspaper covers the entire Central Florida region. The alternative weekly newspaper, *Orlando Weekly* (www.orlandoweekly.com, published Wed., free) is a good resource for arts, entertainment, and dining options, and **Reax** (www.reaxmusic.com, monthly, free) does a great job of covering the regional music scene.

GETTING THERE
By Air
There are two airports that service the greater Orlando area, **Orlando International Airport** (MCO, One Airport Blvd., Orlando, 407/825-2001, www.orlandoairports.net) and **Orlando-Sanford International Airport** (SFB, 1200 Red Cleveland Blvd., Sanford, 407/585-4000, www.orlandosanfordairport.com). The former is one of the busiest airports in the United States and is served by major American and international carriers. The airport in Sanford is used primarily for charter flights, although one low-cost carrier, Allegiant Air, has regularly scheduled year-round service from several U.S. destinations; additionally, Icelandair as well as Scottish low-cost carrier Flyglobespan offer a few international options.

By Car
The only major interstate in the Orlando area is I-4, which connects Daytona Beach (and I-95) and Tampa (and I-75). Orlando is approximately 52 miles (45 minutes' drive) from Daytona and about 86 miles (75 minutes) from Tampa.

There are several toll roads in the area, including State Road 528, a.k.a. the "Beach Line Expressway" that connects Orlando and Cocoa Beach; State Road 417, which is a bypass route that connects Sanford in the north to Disney World in the south; and State Road 408, which bisects central Orlando running east to west.

GETTING AROUND
Orlando is very much a car city, and public transportation here is abysmal. There are bike lanes on most major roads, but cyclists should also know that Orlando is routinely ranked among the most dangerous cities in the United States for cyclists and pedestrians. Parking, however, isn't much of a problem anywhere other than downtown, although there are several new parking garages in the area, and fleets of pedicabs are often hovering outside the garages' exits. Taxi cabs are difficult to hail curbside but are just a phone call away; try **Yellow Cab** (407/422-2222).

Central Florida

The area beyond the busy environs of Orlando offers Old Florida charm and rural beauty. Less than an hour's drive from the skyscrapers and suburbs you can find artists communities, quaint college towns, antiques districts, and even a town filled with spiritualists and psychics.

DELAND

The small town of DeLand is one of the prettiest towns in Central Florida, and it is home to the faith-based Stetson University and a tidy and picturesque downtown. A few minutes from central DeLand is the natural beauty of DeLeon Springs State Park, and if you're in the mood to get your palm read, you can take a quick drive to the spiritualist community of Cassadaga.

Downtown DeLand

The quaint and eminently walkable downtown area of DeLand isn't exactly bursting with activity, but it offers a number of interesting and historical sights. The **Henry A. DeLand House** (137 W. Michigan Ave.) was built in 1886 on land purchased from the town's founding father; currently the building houses a small museum that traces the history of the town. Although Henry DeLand never lived there (his attorney did), later residents included John Stetson, the hatmaker whose name graces **Stetson University** (421 N. Woodland Blvd.). The private Baptist-affiliated college was originally founded by Henry DeLand as DeLand Academy in 1883, but the name was changed in 1889 to honor the generous donations of Stetson, who had to step in with money after Henry DeLand went broke guaranteeing his farmers' citrus crops in a year of a hard freeze. The small tree-lined campus is both picturesque and friendly.

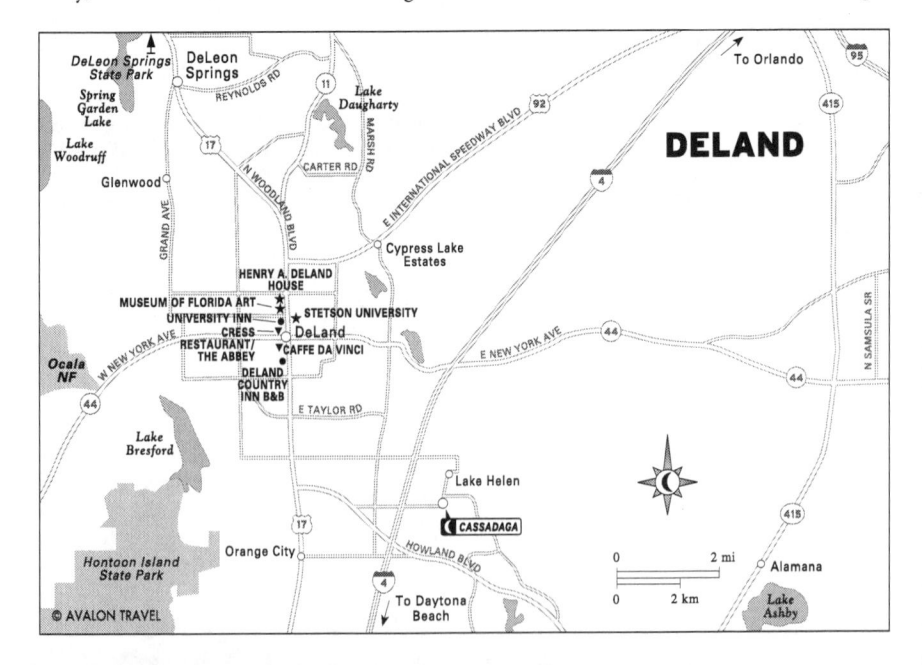

The **Museum of Florida Art** (600 N. Woodland Blvd., 386/734-4371, 10 A.M.–4 P.M. Tues.–Sat., 1–4 P.M. Sun., free) is located right at the edge of the Stetson campus; the small museum's name may be a little misleading considering the limited collections on display, but there are often interesting exhibits of contemporary artists to be found here.

DeLeon Springs State Park

Although recreation areas pop up around many of Florida's natural springs, there are none that can claim what DeLeon Springs State Park (601 Ponce DeLeon Blvd., DeLeon Springs, 386/985-4212, 8 A.M.–sunset daily, $5 per vehicle for up to 8 people) can: a restaurant where you can make your own pancakes at your table. The dining at the **Old Spanish Sugar Mill and Griddle House** is probably as much a draw for visitors as the 72-degree waters; waitstaff bring batter made from stone-ground grains to your griddle-equipped table, and you just add the fruit, chocolate chips, peanut butter, or whatever else you need to make the just-perfect pancake. Of course, activities in the large recreation area are a draw as well, but like many such developed swimming springs, the atmosphere is more like a public pool than a dip into nature's mystery. For that, there are ecotours and canoe or kayak rentals that will get you back into the Lake Woodruff National Wildlife Refuge, home to dozens of bird species and ample fishing opportunities.

◖ Cassadaga

Between DeLand and Orlando is the community of Cassadaga, also known as the "Psychic Center of the World." Such a title isn't bestowed idly, and Cassadaga more than lives up to, and trades off, its reputation as a home of spiritualists, psychics, mediums, and healers. The **Cassadaga Spiritualist Camp** (1112 Steven St., Cassadaga, 386/228-2280, www.cassadaga.org) traces its history back to the 1875 arrival of George P. Colby, a New Yorker who traveled around the country impressing people with his various healing and clairvoyant powers. Guided to this part of Central Florida by Seneca, his Native American spirit guide, Colby established the spiritualist community at Cassadaga in 1894. Today, the

DeLeon Springs State Park

57-acre "camp" (there is no actual camping here) is home to a few hundred permanent residents but sees a near-constant influx of true believers, curious onlookers, and folks just looking for a little spiritual comfort. Healers and mediums will analyze and attempt to correct your spiritual and physical ailments...for a price, of course. It looks just like a regular little community with some turn-of-the-20th-century buildings, houses, and shops, except as anyone of the camp's residents will tell you, there's always more than meets the eye.

Accommodations

DeLand is pretty tiny, and the centrally located **University Inn** (644 N. Woodland Blvd., 386/734-5711, www.universityinndeland.com, from $85 d) will put you across from Stetson and blocks from downtown. With basic clean motel accommodations, it's nothing fancy, but it puts you within walking distance of most of the town's sights. On the opposite end of downtown but still within walking distance of Woodland Avenue's shops and restaurants is the charming and super-friendly **DeLand Country Inn Bed & Breakfast** (228 W. Howry Ave., 386/736-4244, www.delandcountryinn.com, from $89 d). Operated by a British couple, the inn has five spacious and bright bedrooms, two of which share a bathroom, and serves up a gut-busting English breakfast that puts the croissants and coffee at many bed-and-breakfasts to shame.

Food and Drink

Cress Restaurant (103 W. Indiana Ave., 386/734-3740, main courses from $14) offers contemporary global-inspired cuisine in a fine-dining atmosphere. Chef Hari Pulapaka hails from Mumbai, and his delicate touches of chutneys, peppers, and curries don't turn the steak, poultry, and seafood dishes at Cress into Indian food, but they do provide plenty of interesting flavor combinations. The inclusion of unusual dishes like ostrich loin and shiitake-infused grits also adds a bit of adventure to the menu, while the abundance of vegetables and herbs from Cress's organic garden ensure plenty of freshness.

The Abbey (117 N. Woodland Ave., 386/734-4545, 4 P.M.–1 A.M. Mon.–Thurs., 4 P.M.–2 A.M. Fri.–Sat.) offers an excellent selection of imported and microbrewed beers. The classy and comfortable bar area is a great place to get a lesson in Belgian ales, but the sidewalk tables provide an ideal setting to relax and watch small-town DeLand slowly roll by.

Bands from DeLand and Orlando frequently perform at **Caffe Da Vinci** (112 W. Georgia Ave., 386/736-4646, 5 P.M.–2 A.M. Tues.–Fri., noon–2 A.M. Sat.), and the lineups here are often unpredictable; it could be a headbanging metal act or a sensitive singer-songwriter dishing out their tunes onstage. If the band inside isn't your thing, head to the quaint antique-strewn courtyard area to enjoy your coffee or imported beer.

Getting There and Around

DeLand is 38 miles (45 minutes' drive) north of downtown Orlando via I-4. The community of Cassadaga is about 10 miles (10 minutes) south of DeLand.

◖ MOUNT DORA

The primary attraction in Mount Dora is its quaint village atmosphere. The gentle inclines of the town's downtown streets are about as close to "hilly" as one is likely to get in Central Florida, and they don't pose any challenge to the flocks of antique-shoppers and casual strollers who descend on the town every weekend to take in the small-town vibe.

Sights

The cute **Inland Lakes Railway** (150 W. 3rd Ave., departures every 2 hours 11 A.M.–5 P.M. Sat., $12 adults, $10 seniors, $8 children) gives visitors an opportunity to take a brief 75-minute ride on the Mount Dora Champion from the downtown train station, along the banks of Lake Dora, and into the nearby town of Tavares; the train then turns around and comes back. It's not the most exciting voyage in the world, but young kids will certainly get a thrill from riding these rails.

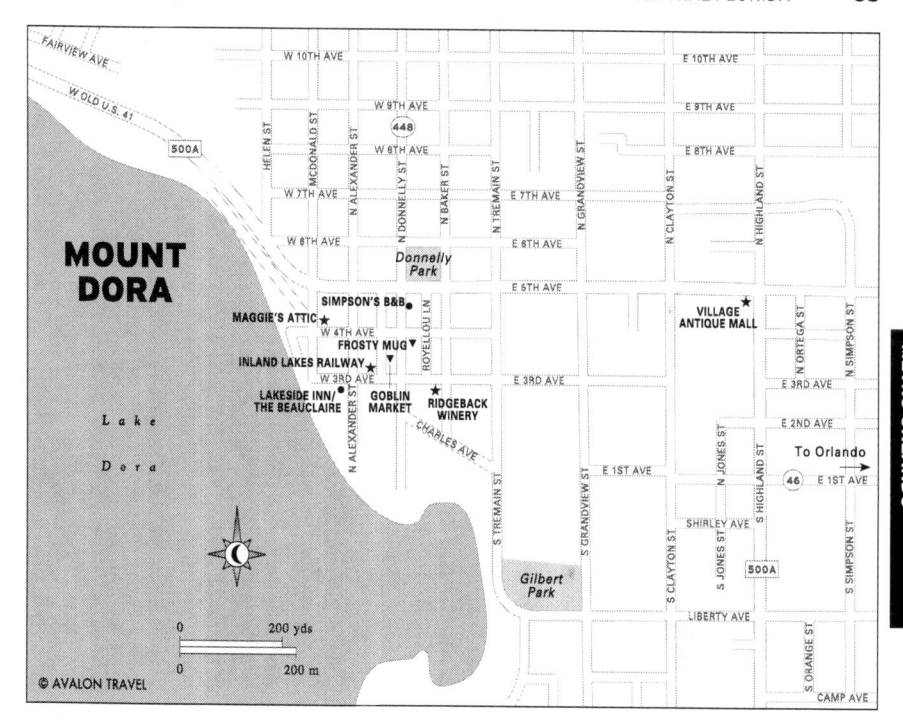

Captain Doolittle's Eco-Tours (dock across from the Lakeside Inn, 352/434-8040, 10 A.M. and 2 P.M. Mon.–Fri., 11 A.M. and 2 P.M. Sat.–Sun.) don't feel all that "eco-friendly" as you putter along the waters of the Harris Chain of Lakes in a covered, 30-passenger boat. However, thanks to guides who know the waters well, you'll be able to spot a variety of wildlife along the banks, ranging from alligators and turtles to hawks, eagles, and other birds.

If the scores of benches strategically placed around Mount Dora aren't relaxing enough, the spacious and verdant **Donnelly Park** (N. Donnelly St. at E. 5th Ave.) is located in the heart of downtown, giving day-trippers and locals alike a place to rest their shopped-out feet.

Shopping

Most visitors make their way to Mount Dora for one of two reasons: They either want to soak up the old-timey vibe, or they want to soak up the bargains in the many antiques shops and boutiques. No shop sums up the adorable factor of Mount Dora more succinctly than **Piglet's Pantry** (400 N. Donnelly St., 352/735-9779, 10 A.M.–5 P.M. Mon.–Sat., 11 A.M.–5 P.M. Sun.), a bakery dedicated to dog treats. If the offerings at the Pantry strike you as too specific, the 70-vendor **Country Cottage Crafts** (334 N. Donnelly St., 352/735-2722, 10 A.M.–6 P.M. daily) features the work of local crafts-makers, with an emphasis on pottery. Similarly, the 12,000-square-foot **Village Antique Mall** (405 Highland St., 352/385-0257, 10 A.M.–6 P.M. daily) is home to the wares of more than 80 local antiques vendors.

The tasting room for the local **Ridgeback Winery** (301 N. Baker St., Suite 104, 352/383-4133, 11 A.M.–5 P.M. Wed.–Sun.) offers a pleasant spot to unwind after a hard day of browsing; Ridgeback's wines are made from grapes bought from other vineyards and then crafted into their own unique blends.

If, however, you're in need of liquid refreshment but haven't yet shopped till you dropped, **Maggie's Attic** (237 W. 4th Ave., Suite 2, 352/383-5451, 10 A.M.–5 P.M. Sun.–Thurs., 10 A.M.–9 P.M. Fri.–Sat.) is part beer and wine bar, part antiques store.

Accommodations

The large **Lakeside Inn** (100 N. Alexander St., 352/383-4101, www.lakeside-inn.com, from $139 d) overlooks Lake Dora and boasts a century-plus history to go along with its commanding views. In addition to historic guests like Thomas Edison and Calvin Coolidge, who dedicated the Gables and Terrace buildings the year after he retired from the White House, one of the oddest visitors to the hotel was an elephant brought in and trained to water-ski for a scene in John Schlesinger's 1981 film *Honky Tonk Freeway*. While some of the 86 guest rooms justifiably creak with age, the trapped-in-amber charm of the Inn is undeniable and irresistible to the antiques shoppers who descend on Mount Dora.

The six-room **Simpson's Bed & Breakfast** (441 N. Donnelly St., 352/383-2087, www.simpsonsbnb.com, from $130 d) is in the heart of downtown Mount Dora. There are two three-room suites and four two-room suites; all the suites have mini-kitchens and are decorated simply, though a bit heavy-handed with the floral patterns. Still, the location can't be beat, as you'll be within two or three blocks of almost everything Mount Dora has to offer.

Food and Drink

The Beauclaire (100 N. Alexander St., 352/383-4101, 7 A.M.–10 P.M. Mon.–Sat., 7 A.M.–2:30 P.M. Sun., main courses from $19) acts as the main dining room at the Lakeside Inn, but its Southern charm and easy elegance make it a local favorite. The traditional American fare of steaks, chops, and poultry is far from adventurous, but the sunset views are tough to beat.

True adventurers should head for the **Frosty Mug** (100 E. 4th Ave., 352/383-1696, 11 A.M.–9 P.M. Sun.–Thurs., 11 A.M.–10 P.M. Fri.–Sat., main courses from $12), a Viking-themed restaurant in the heart of downtown. Yes, Viking-themed. Although only a few dishes—haddock, smoked salmon—reflect the Icelandic implications of the name, the menu is rounded out by steaks, meat loaf, chicken, and a handful of German specialties (schnitzel, bratwurst). Upstairs is the Viking Lounge, which is really just a nice bar with a Viking helmet or two.

The fresh salads and piled-high sandwiches draw a lunch crowd to the **Goblin Market** (330 Dora Drawdy Way, 352/735-0059, lunch 11 A.M.–3 P.M. Tues.–Sat., noon–4 P.M. Sun., dinner 5–9 P.M. Tues.–Thurs., 5–10 P.M. Fri.–Sat., main courses from $10), but it's the European-inspired dinner menu—escargot, shrimp, and scallop fra diavolo, Gouda-stuffed chicken breast—that's worthy of a late-evening look. The dark and labyrinthine dining room feels more like a quirky salon than a four-star restaurant.

Getting There and Around

Mount Dora is about 30 miles (an hour's drive) southwest of DeLand via scenic State Road 44. Coming from Orlando, the 27-mile, 45-minute drive on U.S. 441 will take you through some of Orlando's bland suburbs before the rolling hills of Apopka and Zellwood put you in an appropriately rural mood.

Part of the joy of visiting Mount Dora is simply walking around and exploring the downtown area, but for those less inclined to wear out the soles of their shoes, guided tours can be had via **Segway of Central Florida** (140 W. 5th Ave., 352/383-9900, 1-hour tours $48) or the **Mt. Dora Trolley Co.** (departs from Lakeside Inn hourly 11 A.M.–2 P.M. daily, $13 adults, $11 children).

Acknowledgments

This book makes reference to various Disney copyrighted characters, trademarks, marks, and registered marks owned by The Walt Disney Company and Disney Enterprises, Inc. including:

Adventureland®
Cirque du Soleil® show La Nouba™
Conservation Station®
Discovery Island®
DisneyQuest®
Disney's Animal Kingdom® Theme Park
Disney's Hollywood Studios® Theme Park
Downtown Disney®
Epcot®
Expedition Everest™
Fantasyland®
Frontierland®
Indiana Jones™ Epic Stunt Spectacular
It's Tough to be a Bug®
Kali River Rapids®
Kilimanjaro Safaris®
Magic Kingdom® Park
Maharajah Jungle Trek®
Main Street, U.S.A.®
Mickey's Toontown® Fair
Pangani Forest Exploration Trail®
Primeval Whirl®
Rafiki's Planet Watch®
Rock 'n Roller Coaster®
Soarin'™
Space Mountain®
Stitch's Great Escape!™
The Boneyard®
The Twilight Zone Tower of Terror™
Tomorrowland®
Tree of Life® Attraction
Walt Disney
Walt Disney World® Resort

www.moon.com

DESTINATIONS | ACTIVITIES | BLOGS | MAPS | BOOKS

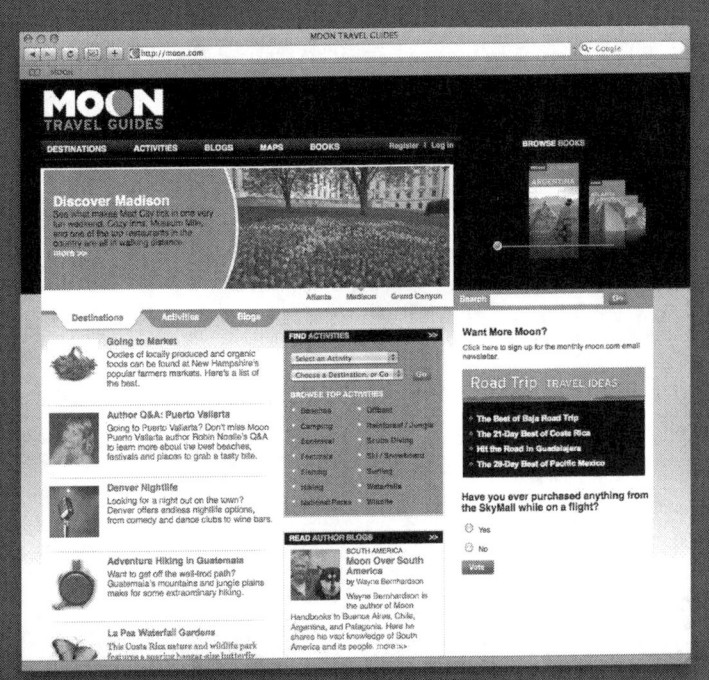

MOON.COM is ready to help plan your next trip! Filled with fresh trip ideas and strategies, author interviews, informative travel blogs, a detailed map library, and descriptions of all the Moon guidebooks, Moon.com is all you need to get out and explore the world—or even places in your own backyard. While at Moon.com, sign up for our monthly e-newsletter for updates on new releases, travel tips, and expert advice from our on-the-go Moon authors. As always, when you travel with Moon, expect an experience that is uncommon and truly unique.

MOON IS ON FACEBOOK—BECOME A FAN!
JOIN THE MOON PHOTO GROUP ON FLICKR

MAP SYMBOLS

▬▬▬	Expressway	🄲	Highlight	✈	Airfield	⛳	Golf Course
▬▬▬	Primary Road	○	City/Town	✈	Airport	🅿	Parking Area
▬▬▬	Secondary Road	⦿	State Capital	▲	Mountain	▰	Archaeological Site
▭▭▭	Unpaved Road	⊛	National Capital	✢	Unique Natural Feature	⛪	Church
-------	Trail	★	Point of Interest			⛽	Gas Station
·········	Ferry	•	Accommodation	𓄃	Waterfall	◌	Glacier
─ ─ ─	Railroad	▼	Restaurant/Bar	♠	Park	🟫	Mangrove
▨▨▨	Pedestrian Walkway	■	Other Location	🄷	Trailhead	▨▨	Reef
▥▥▥	Stairs	⋀	Campground	⛷	Skiing Area	▱	Swamp

CONVERSION TABLES

°C = (°F - 32) / 1.8
°F = (°C x 1.8) + 32
1 inch = 2.54 centimeters (cm)
1 foot = 0.304 meters (m)
1 yard = 0.914 meters
1 mile = 1.6093 kilometers (km)
1 km = 0.6214 miles
1 fathom = 1.8288 m
1 chain = 20.1168 m
1 furlong = 201.168 m
1 acre = 0.4047 hectares
1 sq km = 100 hectares
1 sq mile = 2.59 square km
1 ounce = 28.35 grams
1 pound = 0.4536 kilograms
1 short ton = 0.90718 metric ton
1 short ton = 2,000 pounds
1 long ton = 1.016 metric tons
1 long ton = 2,240 pounds
1 metric ton = 1,000 kilograms
1 quart = 0.94635 liters
1 US gallon = 3.7854 liters
1 Imperial gallon = 4.5459 liters
1 nautical mile = 1.852 km

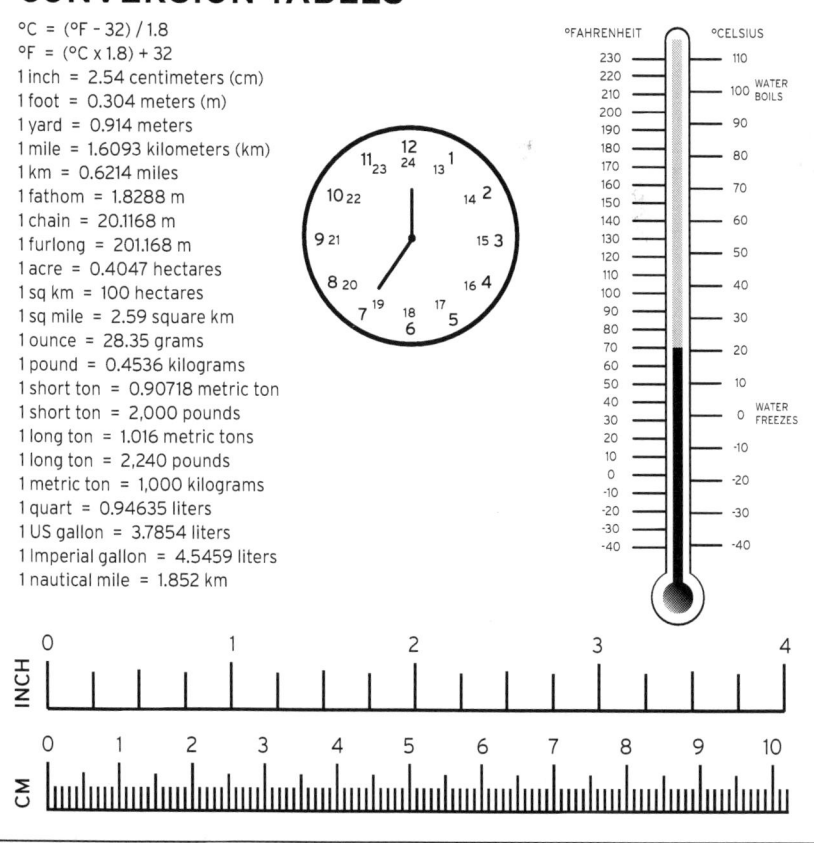

MOON SPOTLIGHT
WALT DISNEY WORLD & ORLANDO
Avalon Travel
a member of the Perseus Books Group
1700 Fourth Street
Berkeley, CA 94710, USA
www.moon.com

Editor and Series Manager: Kathryn Ettinger
Copy Editor: Christopher Church
Graphics Coordinator: Sean Bellows
Production Coordinator: Domini Dragoone
Cover Designer: Domini Dragoone
Map Editor: Mike Morgenfeld
Cartographers: Kat Bennett, Chris Markiewicz
Proofreader: Nikki Iokimedes

ISBN: 978-1-59880-835-3

Text © 2011 by Jason Ferguson.
Maps © 2011 by Avalon Travel.
All rights reserved.

Some photos and illustrations are used by permission and are the property of the original copyright owners.

Front cover photo: Spaceship Earth at Epcot, Walt Disney World, © Walt Disney World®
Title page photo: Fireworks over Cinderella Castle at the Magic Kingdom, Walt Disney World, © Kjersti Jorgensen/123rf.com

Printed in the United States

Moon Spotlight and the Moon logo are the property of Avalon Travel. All other marks and logos depicted are the property of the original owners. All rights reserved. No part of this book may be translated or reproduced in any form, except brief extracts by a reviewer for the purpose of a review, without written permission of the copyright owner.

All recommendations, including those for sights, activities, hotels, restaurants, and shops, are based on each author's individual judgment. We do not accept payment for inclusion in our travel guides, and our authors don't accept free goods or services in exchange for positive coverage.

Although every effort was made to ensure that the information was correct at the time of going to press, the author and publisher do not assume and hereby disclaim any liability to any party for any loss or damage caused by errors, omissions, or any potential travel disruption due to labor or financial difficulty, whether such errors or omissions result from negligence, accident, or any other cause.

ABOUT THE AUTHOR

Jason Ferguson

Florida native Jason Ferguson has yet to find a corner of his home state that doesn't hold some sort of surprise. With a background in alternative journalism and arts and culture reporting, Jason enjoys discovering some of Florida's more unusual sights and diverse nightlife and art scenes. As a father of two, he also understands the infinite appeal of Florida's theme parks, beaches, and outdoor opportunities.

Jason has written for publications ranging from *Time Out, Travel + Leisure,* and *Caribbean Travel & Life* to Florida newspapers such as the *Orlando Weekly* and *Miami New Times*. He enjoys sniffing out the beauty of Florida's natural history as well as the oddness of its quirky present. He, his wife, and their two kids utilize their home in Central Florida as a launching pad for weekend adventures that take them to points of interest throughout the state. Although their favorite spots change from week to week, there's a general consensus that a life without the pancakes from the Old Spanish Sugar Mill and Griddle House restaurant at DeLeon Springs State Park is a life not worth living.